a **WEE GUIDE** *to*

Scottish History

Martin Coventry

GOBLINSHEAD

Edinburgh

a **WEE GUIDE** to Scottish History

First Published 1996
Reprinted 1997,1999
© Martin Coventry 1996
Published by **GOBLINSHEAD**
130B Inveresk Road
Musselburgh EH21 7AY
Scotland
tel 0131 665 2894; *fax* 0131 653 6566
email goblinshead@sol.co.uk

British Library Cataloguing in Publication Data
A catalogue record for this book is available from the British Library.

ISBN 1 899874 01 1

Typeset by **GOBLINSHEAD** using Desktop Publishing
Typeset in Garamond Narrow

WEE GUIDES
William Wallace
The Picts
Scottish History
The Jacobites
Robert Burns
Mary, Queen of Scots
Robert the Bruce
Haunted Castles of Scotland
Old Churches and Abbeys of Scotland
Castles and Mansions of Scotland
New for 1999
Prehistoric Scotland
Macbeth and Early Scotland
Whisky

a **WEE GUIDE** *to*
Scottish History

Contents

List of maps

List of illustrations

All photos and maps by Martin Coventry, except for front cover illustration by Joyce Miller.

Acknowledgements

Thanks very much to everyone who helped get this book from a vague idea into its finished form.

Particular thanks to Dr Fiona Watson, at Stirling University, and to Dilys Jones, who read over the text; to Joyce Miller, who checked the places to visit as well as much much more, and to Aileen Turnbull, who phoned many attractions for details. Also to Gillian at Dillons and Alex at Waterstones in Glasgow, and to Joe at Waterstones in Edinburgh.

How to use this book

This book is divided into three parts:

- **ANCIENT TIMES:** The first part (pages 2–19) covers from about 5000 BC to 1066 AD, with a map (page 2). Places to visit are listed at the end of this part (page 13) with a map (page 12).
- **MIDDLE AGES:** The second part (pages 20–65) covers from 1066 to 1689, with maps (pages 20, 26, 32 & 38). Places to visit are listed at the end of this part with maps (pages 46 & 54), divided into Churches & Abbeys (page 47); and Castles (page 55).
- **MODERN TIMES:** The third part (pages 66–87) covers from 1690 to the present – and a bit beyond – with maps (pages 66 & 70). Places to visit are listed at the end of this part (page 79) with a map (page 78).

An index (pages 88-9) lists all the main people, battles and events, while the Places to Visit index (page 90) is arranged alphabetically.

PLACES TO VISIT: The entries for the places to visit consist of the map reference number – which locates the place on the map at the beginning of each places to visit chapter – name, National Grid reference, OS sheet number. This is followed by basic directions, a brief description of the attraction, and the telephone number and opening – where appropriate. The entry is concluded by a list of facilities, including parking, refreshments, sales area, WC, admission, and disabled facilities.

Warning

While the information in this book was believed to be correct at time of going to press – and was checked, where possible, with the visitor attractions – opening times and facilities, or other information, may vary or differ from that included. All information should be checked with the visitor attractions before embarking on any journey. Inclusion in the text is no indication whatsoever that a site is open to the public or that it should be visited. Many sites, particularly prehistoric sites and ruined castles, are potentially dangerous and great care should be taken: the publisher and author cannot accept responsibility for damage or injury caused from any visit. Or paper cuts from opening the book.

The places listed to visit are only a personal selection of what is available in Scotland, and the inclusion or exclusion of a visitor attraction in the text should not be considered as a comment or judgement on that attraction.

Locations on maps are approximate.

Introduction

Many years ago I studied history at school, but gave it up as soon as possible. The past, even Scotland's, held little interest – it seemed dull, dreary and disjointed: one week we would cover Robert the Bruce, the next week Bonnie Prince Charlie – without any idea what happened before, between and after. There was nothing to get your teeth into. I went on to do subjects with a more practical feel, such as physics and chemistry, and then studied engineering at college.

When a teenager I had read *Lord of the Rings* by J R R Tolkien, but I never thought *real* history could be as fascinating as the deeds of Frodo Baggins and Gandalf and Sauron. Then I read more about my own country, and realized that Scotland's past was every bit as powerful and interesting as a Tolkien epic. There were dark deeds, battles, struggles against vastly superior forces, a few heroes, far more villains, and a vast rush of time carrying me from the inhabitants of Skara Brae right to the present. I hope this wee book relates some of that fascination and enthusiasm.

My own favourite story did not make it into the text, but I will tell it here. Earl Sigurd slew Maelbrigit, mormaer of Moray, beheading him and tying the head to his saddle. Sigurd was riding home when the movement of his horse caused Maelbrigit's severed head to bite his leg. The Earl died from the resultant wound, probably by blood poisoning.

I hope the following book gives the reader a taste for Scotland's past, and I have not let the facts spoil a wonderful history.

MC, Edinburgh, November 1996

Map 1: Ancient Times

SHETLAND

• **Lerwick**
• Clickhimin

• Mousa

ORKNEY
• Knap of Howar

Midhowe •
Skara Brae •   • Gurness
Ring of Brodgar
Stones of Steness   • **Kirkwall**
Maes Howe

Thurso

Dun Dornaigil
• **Wick**

Dun Carloway •   LEWIS

• Callanish
Stornoway

HARRIS

NORTH
UIST

• **Ullapool**

Burghead
• **Fraserburgh**

Inverness   MORAY   • **Elgin**
• Sueno's Stone
• Clava Cairns

SOUTH
UIST

SKYE

• Urquhart   PICTS   **Aberdeen**

• Glenelg Brochs   Lumphanan

• BARRA

• **Fort William**   ✕ Mons Graupius (84)

Nechtansmere (685) • **Montrose**

Dunkeld •   Meigle
✕ Aberlemno
Luncarty •   Scone   **Dundee**
Perth •   St Andrews
Forteviot   • Abernethy   FIFE

MULL
Iona ◯   • Dunstaffnage
Oban

• Dunadd
JURA   DALRIADA

Stirling

Dumbarton •
Rough Cas •   **Edinburgh**
Cairnpapple •   LOTHIAN   • Traprain Law
• Glasgow   FORTH   **Dunbar**

ISLAY

STRATHCLYDE

• **Lanark**

Melrose •   ✕ Carham
Eildon Hill   (1018)

Machrie Moor •
ARRAN   • **Ayr**

CLYDE

ENGLAND

• **Dumfries**

Stranraer •   GALLOWAY

• Whithorn

PART ONE: ANCIENT TIMES

The First Peoples

5000 BC First people arrive (Middle Stone Age – Mesolithic)

Not much is known about the first settlers who came to Scotland. Evidence is restricted to tools, weapons and middens. These first incomers were nomads, who lived in caves or rough shelters, and used stone implements. They ate what they could find or catch: deer, eggs, berries, nuts and often shell-fish – some of their middens contain millions of shells. Beyond the coast were forests covering much of the land, so they travelled by boat as journeys by foot would have been slow, difficult and possibly dangerous.

5000–2300 BC First people settle (New Stone Age – Neolithic)

About 4000 BC, settlers began to arrive and farm in Scotland, bringing with them domestic animals, such as cattle, sheep, goats and pigs; and cereal crops, such as wheat and barley. This new way of life involved forest clearance, although these settlers also depended on hunting and fishing. Stone and flint were used for tools and weapons; and they were skilled at making decorated pots, many of which have been found in their tombs.

Their settlements have left little or no trace – apart from in a few caves – except in Orkney, where there are remains of early Neolithic stone houses at Skara Brae and Knap of Howar.

These dwellings are built of fine drystone masonry and have central hearths. Fittings included dressers, beds and boxes, all carefully fashioned from stone.

These settlers built elaborate chambered tombs, covered by a cairn of stones, to bury their dead. These

Skara Brae

cairns take many different forms, some having a single chamber, reached by a passageway, with smaller chambers off; some having a longer chamber, divided by stone slabs into stalls.

The best example of a chambered cairn is at Maes Howe, and there are many other fine examples of both chambered and stalled cairns in Orkney. Practices in burying the dead seem to have varied with place and time: in some the remains were cremated before being buried; in others the body was simply interred; while in others thigh bones or skulls were collected together.

These tombs were used for hundreds of years, previous burials often being moved aside. Pottery and grave goods were also buried with the bodies, and in some of the tombs in Orkney the remains of oxen, dogs or sea-eagles have also been found.

The settlers of this time also erected standing stones and stone circles, such as those at Machrie Moor, and the Stones of Steness: a henge monument, consisting of a circle surrounded by a ditch. In some cases, these stones were decorated with cup and ring marks, which are also found in many other places throughout Scotland.

2300–500 BC Copper and bronze come into use (Bronze Age)

Trade developed between the settlers in Scotland and the rest of the British Isles and the Continent, and there appears to have been a relatively large and increasing population.

By this time, copper or bronze weapons and implements had begun to be used, although many were still made of wood or bone. Gold was also used for decorative items, such as armlets, cloak pins and dress fasteners. Many artefacts survive from this period as copper, bronze and gold do not corrode as readily as iron.

These people lived in round houses, which now only survive as hut circles, or indentations, in the ground. The walls were either of turf or stone, and a wooden post held up a thatched roof. A central hearth contained a fire for cooking and warmth. Remains of their field systems also survive, as do the heaps of stones which were removed to improve fields for ploughing.

Burials were now in a cist, or stone box, with a stone lid. The body was placed in the grave in a crouched position, usually with a food pot. Cremations replaced inhumations towards the end of the Bronze Age, the burnt bones being deposited in cinerary urns, many of which survive. This pottery is of a characteristic type, hard and thin, red in colour, and decorated with a tooth-like ornamentation. Some have distinguished these settlers as the *Beaker People*, suggesting they were incomers from the Continent.

Many stone circles were built, or rebuilt at the same site, including the large circle at the Ring of Brodgar, the stones at Callanish, and some of the circles at Machrie Moor. Other sites were used for burials, cairns being built within the circles, such as at Clava Cairns and Cairnpapple Hill.

1000–400 BC Influx of Celtic peoples & the Iron Age

Around 1000 BC the climate seems to have deteriorated, and become colder and wetter. About this time, the first Celtic peoples arrived in Scotland, people who may have shared a common language and religion. They built hill forts and lived in enclosed settlements, and their societies seem to have been divided into families or clans, led by a chief or king.

There are many hill forts throughout Scotland. Often these consist of a series of ramparts surrounding a hill or cutting off a promontory; or alternatively drystone walls, without mortar, were built, some with a timber frame. Some of these enclosures are small, and would hold no more than one family; while others, such as those at Eildon Hill or Traprain Law, could contain a whole town, with workshops as well as houses.

Callanish (see previous page)

These forts were probably more to protect against a sudden onslaught, rather than a protracted siege, as many have no apparent water supplies. Others are in very poor defensive sites. Crannogs, small defensive settlements on islands in lochs, natural or man-made, were also used during this time.

The inhabitants were farmers as well as warriors, and had domesticated animals, including horses, cattle, pigs, sheep and goats. They also grew cereals, such as barley, and vegetables, such as peas. Iron was smelted and forged into weapons and tools from about 500 BC, wool was spun and woven into cloth, and bone was still used for small items such as needles and combs.

Because iron corrodes readily, there are far fewer iron artefacts dating from this period than copper or bronze items from the Bronze Age.

400 BC–200 AD Duns & Brochs

Hill forts were still built and occupied at this time, but other defensive structures, brochs and duns, were also developed.

Brochs were tall, round drystone towers. The walls had a gallery running up inside them, with a stair or storage area. There was only one low entrance, defended by a drawbar and guardroom. The sites were sometimes further strengthened by a series of ramparts, including a blockhouse, in front of the entrance. Like castles, brochs were permanently occupied and do not appear to have been built just for refuge. Many have wells or a water tanks built into the floor, and they may have had a timber roof.

The best surviving example is that at Mousa in Shetland, although there are other well-preserved brochs at Dun Carloway, Dun Troddan and Dun Telve at Glenelg, Dun Dornaigil, Clickhimin, Midhowe and Gurness.

Settlements built up around brochs, and were occupied and modified over many centuries. What is not clear is what brochs were built to defend against: rival families and clans, or invaders and pirates, or Roman slave ships.

Duns closely resemble brochs in the type of construction, and

Dun Carloway

were simple stone enclosures, surrounding a defensible rock, or cutting off a headland.

By about 100 BC, these tribes or clans were in two rough groups: the Picts, north of the Forth-Clyde valley; and the Britons to the south and into most of England. Their societies were complex, artistic and probably war-like, no longer purely farmers, with carpenters and masons, metal-workers and merchants, ruled over by a chief or dynasty. They were druids and pagans, although little is known of their beliefs except what was recorded by the Romans.

79–84 AD The coming of the Romans & Battle of Mons Graupius

After successfully invading the south of England from 55 BC under Julius Caesar, the Romans moved north. In 79 AD Julius Agricola, Roman governor of Britain, advanced into Scotland, and built forts at strategic positions. He crushed any opposition, but the Caledonians – as the Romans called them – with a major fortress called Alcluyd at Dumbarton Rock, resisted him. Another invasion by the Romans in 82 AD was followed a year later by the slaughter of the Ninth Roman Legion, probably in Galloway.

At the Battle of Mons Graupius in 84 AD the Caledonians suffered a terrible defeat. Their chief Calgacus, if the chronicler Tactius is to be believed, is the first named *Scot* in history. Calgacus was slain at the battle, along with 10 000 of his men, while only 340 Roman soldiers were killed. Although this defeat was a major setback for the Caledonian tribes, the Romans found it difficult to consolidate their victory.

120–208 AD Hadrian's Wall & Antonine's Wall

The northern Caledonian tribes continued to be so troublesome that the Emperor Hadrian had a wall built to keep them from attacking the Roman Province of Britain to the south. Hadrian's Wall stretched across the country, from Newcastle, on the east side of England, to Bowness, on the southern shore of the Solway Firth. The wall was built of stone, and many forts and outposts were constructed along its length.

The Romans invaded again in 139 AD under Lollius Ubricus. They built another wall, Antonine's Wall, between the Forth and the Clyde in an attempt to consolidate their hold on southern Scotland. However, they were soon pushed back to Hadrian's Wall, despite the efforts of the Second, Sixth and 20th Legions to provide the emperor with a victory. In 208, the Romans, this time under Lucius Septimus Severus, attacked again after an uprising by the Caledonian tribes. But his force was harried relentlessly and was soon forced to retreat.

The best surviving section of Antonine's Wall is at Rough Castle near Falkirk, and parts of Hadrian's Wall and some of the forts in Northumberland are also open to the public.

296–360 AD Picts & Scots

The Picts were first mentioned by the Romans as the people who held the north and east of Scotland. Little is known of them or of their language – as with all those who came before them – and the lasting remnant of their culture is restricted to carved symbol stones, a collection of which can be found at Meigle, as well as outstanding examples at Aberlemno and Sueno's Stone in Moray. The Picts were probably a Celtic people, more akin to the Britons and the Gaels than to the Teutonic Saxons.

The Scots, from the north part of Ireland, were first mentioned about 360 AD by the Romans, although they did not use this name themselves. After the withdrawal of the Roman legions from Britain, in 368 the Picts and Scots, along with the Saxons, attacked the south, ravaged the Roman province of Britain, and plundered London of its riches.

Little of Roman culture, learning or influence survived in Scotland.

Sueno's Stone (and protective canopy)

The Making of the Kingdom

400 Picts & Britons

With the withdrawal of the Roman legions, the Picts controlled the east and north, and were divided into the north Picts, and the south Picts in Galloway. The north Picts may have had their capital at Inverness, but also had important centres at Burghead, Urquhart – later used as a castle in medieval times – Dunkeld, Scone, Forteviot and Abernethy. The Picts spoke Britonnic Gaelic, akin to the Welsh language, and used matrilineal descent of inheritance for their kings, where the line descended through the mother.

Strathclyde was occupied by the Britons, whose kingdom at one time stretched from Cornwall, through Wales and Cumbria, to Dumbarton. The Britons also spoke a language related to Welsh.

These kingdoms, and the later realms of the Scots and Angles, spent much of their time, and vigour, fighting each other.

430 St Ninian & St Patrick

By 430, St Ninian, a Briton, had been active in Galloway, converting the south Picts to Christianity, probably to a Roman form of worship. He founded a religious house, *Candida Casa* – so-called because the walls of his church were whitewashed – at Whithorn. Ninian died in 432. Whithorn was a place of pilgrimage in medieval times, and ruins of a 12th-century cathedral church and priory survive. St Ninian's Cave, south-west of Whithorn, is traditionally associated with the saint.

In the same year, St Patrick, said to have been born at Kilpatrick, near Dumbarton, converted many of the Irish to Christianity

500 The coming of the Scots

It was in 503 that many Scots left Ireland and settled in Argyll, either driving out or coming to an arrangement with the Picts. The Scots had raided along the coasts of the south-west for many years. Their kingdom was known as Dalriada, and their king, Fergus MacErc, reputedly brought with him the Stone of Destiny. Dunstaffnage, later used as the site for a medieval castle, and Dunadd, an impressive hill fort, were two of their strongholds. About this time the Scots became Christians.

547 Bernicia & the kingdom of the Angles

The Angles held much of the east of England by 547, and King Ida became the ruler of Bernicia, which included lands from the Firth of Forth to the River Tees, in the north of England. His capital was at Bamburgh – the site of which is occupied by a medieval castle – in Northumberland. The Angles were pagans.

563 St Columba & St Mungo

St Columba, a Scot from Ireland, settled at Iona, bringing with him the Celtic form of the Christian church. He converted the north Picts, ruled by King Brude from a stronghold at or near Inverness, and is said to have confronted a serpent in Loch Ness, the first mention of a monster there. Iona became the centre of Christianity in Scotland. The present restored abbey and nunnery date from medieval times, but many early Scots, Irish and Norse kings are buried here.

About the same time, St Mungo, who is also known as Kentigern, converted the Britons of Strathclyde, and Glasgow Cathedral is dedicated to him. The Cathedral is mainly medieval, but is built over Mungo's tomb.

600 Conversion of the Angles to Christianity

St Aidan, a missionary from Iona, converted the Angles of Bernicia to Christianity, the work being continued by St Cuthbert. Lindisfarne, in Northumberland, became a great religious centre, and the ruins of a later priory are in the care of English Heritage and open to the public.

High Cross, Iona

663 The Celtic Church & the Synod of Whitby

The Synod of Whitby was held, in Yorkshire in England, at which the ritual and beliefs of the Roman Church, particularly the dating of Easter, were asserted over the practices of the Celtic Church. The Roman Church came to dominate the whole of Scotland.

685 Battle of Nechtansmere

The Angles of Bernicia tried to push their border far to the north, but were defeated by the Picts at the Battle of Nechtansmere, near Forfar. Their king, Egfrid, was slain with much of his army. The carved stones at Aberlemno, which are near Nechtansmere, probably commemorate this battle. The Picts extended their influence south again, and dominated the Scottish kingdom of Dalriada.

733 St Andrew, Patron Saint of Scotland

Acca, Bishop of Hexham, brought the relics of St Andrew to Fife, where there was already a religious settlement, probably founded by St Rule, a disciple of Columba, about 590. St Andrews Cathedral, now a fragmentary ruin, was founded on the site of this early community. The flag of Scotland, the white saltire on a

9

blue background, represents the crucifixion of St Andrew on an 'X' shaped cross. One story is that the cross appeared in the sky before a victory by the Scots or Picts over the Norsemen, and this was attributed to the Saint's intercession.

793–826 Lindisfarne & Iona attacked

The Norsemen sacked Lindisfarne in 793, and looted Iona in 795. These attacks forced Iona to be abandoned, and the monks moved to Dunkeld in 826, which was safer from Norse long ships. The partly ruined Cathedral at Dunkeld is built on the site of an earlier church.

The Norsemen raided all along the coasts, and greatly weakened the northern kingdoms. They settled in Orkney and Shetland, and parts of the northern mainland and the western isles, forming a powerful Norse province.

843–59 Union of Scots & Picts – Kenneth MacAlpin

Kenneth MacAlpin united the crowns of the Scots and the Picts. What is unusual about this union is that at this time the Picts had the upper hand in the fighting between the two peoples. The union seems to have been peaceful. Kenneth had a claim to the throne of Picts through his mother, a Pictish princess, although he secured his position by slaughtering all his rivals. Nearly all Pictish culture and language was lost.

Kenneth moved from fortresses at

Dunstaffnage Castle

Dunadd and Dunstaffnage to Dunkeld, Scone and Forteviot, which were much safer from Norse attack.

859–900 Donald I, Constantine I, Aed, Eochaid & Giric, Donald II

Donald I, Kenneth's brother, succeeded to the throne, but died in 863. He was followed by Constantine I, who was slain in battle against the Norsemen in 877; and then Aed, who was killed by his cousin, Giric, in 878. Eochaid the Venomous and Giric ruled as joint monarchs, but in 889 both kings were deposed, and Giric was killed in a siege at the fortress of Dundurn. They were succeeded by Donald II, but he was poisoned in 900.

900–943 Constantine II & the Battle of Brananburgh

Constantine II came to the throne in 900 and ruled for 43 years, a very long reign indeed for the time. The kingdom of Strathclyde had become dependent on the Scots, and in 908 the throne passed to Constantine's brother. Constantine spent much of his reign fighting the Norse and driving them from his realm.

However, in 937, Constantine and the Scots, and an army of Irish and Northumbrian Norsemen and Britons, were defeated by Athelstane, King of the Saxons, with great slaughter of the Scots and their allies. The southern borders of the kingdom of Scots were attacked, and in 943 Constantine resigned his throne to his cousin, Malcolm I.

943–1005 Malcolm I, Indulf, Duff, Culen, Kenneth II, Constantine III, Kenneth III

In return for land, Malcolm I apparently became a vassal of the English king, Athelstane. However, in 950 he captured Northumberland, but was killed in a battle with the men of Moray. He was followed by Indulf, who was probably killed about 962; then Duff, who was slain in Moray in 967; then Culen, who was put down by the Britons in Lothian in 971.

The reign of Kenneth II was relatively peaceful, until he was poisoned in 995 by Finella, whose son had been murdered by Kenneth. It is during his reign that the thistle traditionally became associated with Scotland. At a battle in 973 at Luncarty, the sleeping Scottish forces were woken when the Norse enemy stumbled into a patch of thistles. The first recorded use of the thistle, however, is on coins in the reign of James III in 1470.

Constantine III came to the throne in 995, but was murdered in 997. He was followed by Kenneth III, who was slain in 1005 by Malcolm II.

Dynastic fighting, failed invasions, and Norse raids weakened the kingdom, and by 1005 the Scots had lost control of Lothian and Strathclyde, the north and west were held by the Norsemen, and Moray and other areas were in rebellion.

1005–34 Malcolm II & the Battle of Carham

Malcolm II came to the throne in 1005, and in 1010 he defeated a Norse army at Dufftown and secured his northern border, by a combination of fighting and marrying off his daughter to the Norse Jarl of Orkney. Turning his attention to the south, Malcolm and the Scots, aided by Owen the Bald of Strathclyde, defeated the Saxons, under King Uhtred, at Carham, in 1018, occupying Lothian. Owen was killed at the battle and Strathclyde was absorbed into the kingdom of Scots – which more or less assumed its present southern border.

Malcolm II ensured Duncan's succession by slaughtering other claimants.

1034–58 Duncan & Macbeth

Duncan came to the throne in 1034, but was, in his turn, slain in battle by Macbeth – not in his bed with a bloodied dagger as described by Shakespeare. Macbeth ruled well, strengthening the kingdom sufficiently to make a pilgrimage to Rome in 1050. However, in 1057 he was killed at Lumphanan by Malcolm Canmore – Canmore meaning *big head* – son of Duncan, who was helped by Edward the Confessor of England. Malcolm Canmore – Malcolm III – was named king. Lulach the Fool, a distant relation of Macbeth, was set up as a rival claimant to the throne, but was slain by Malcolm in 1058.

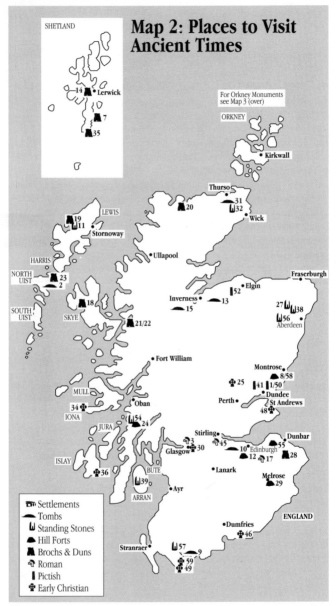

SHETLAND

14 • Lerwick

▲7

▲35

Map 2: Places to Visit Ancient Times

For Orkney Monuments see Map 3 (over)

ORKNEY

• Kirkwall

Thurso
▲20   ▲31
             ⊍32 • Wick

          ▲19
          ⊍11   LEWIS
          • Stornoway

HARRIS

NORTH UIST   ▲23
               ▲2

SOUTH UIST   ▲18   SKYE

                    ▲21/22

          • Ullapool

                              ▲52 • Elgin   Fraserburgh
          • Inverness   — 13   27 ⊍ ▲38
                    — 15   ⊍56
                                        Aberdeen

• Fort William

                          Montrose •
                               ▲8/58
          ✚25 | 41 | 1/50
MULL   Perth • — Dundee
34 ✚   ◈ St Andrews
IONA   • Oban   48 ✚
       ⊍54
JURA   ▲24
              Stirling •   Dunbar
ISLAY   ◈3   ▲10 • 55
        ✚30 ▲45   12 ◈17 ▲28
        Glasgow Edinburgh
                              Melrose
BUTE   ⊍39 • Lanark   ▲29
ARRAN • Ayr

✚36   ENGLAND

              • Dumfries
              ✚46

Stranraer •   ⊍57
              — 9
            ✚59
            49

Key:
- ▥▥ Settlements
- — Tombs
- ⊍ Standing Stones
- ◣ Hill Forts
- ▲ Brochs & Duns
- ◈ Roman
- | Pictish
- ✚ Early Christian

Places to Visit Ancient Times

P	Parking	
S	Sales Area	
🍴	Refreshments	
wc	Toilet	
£	Admission Charge	
&	Disabled	
HS	Historic Scotland	
NTS	National Trust for Scot.	

1 Aberlemno Sculptured Stones

NO 523557 54 HS
Off B9134, 6 miles NE of Forfar, Angus
A magnificent cross-slab with Pictish symbols at Aberlemno, as well as other stones by the road side of the B9314.
Stones covered over in winter
P Nearby

2 Barpa Langass

NF 837657 18
Off A867, 5 miles W of Lochmaddy, North Uist
Impressive chambered cairn, dating from the Neolithic period.
Open all year
P

3 Bearsden Bathhouse

NS 546720 64 HS
Off A809, on Roman Road, Bearsden, nr Glasgow
Remains of Roman bath-house.
Open all year
P Nearby

4 Blackhammer Chambered Cairn

HY 414276 06 HS
On B9065, S of Island of Rousay, Orkney
Long cairn, divided into seven compartments, dating from the Neolithic period.
Open all year

5 Broch of Gurness

HY 383268 06 HS
Off A966,14 miles NW of Kirkwall, Orkney
Impressive broch and settlement, defended by a series of ramparts, near the sea. Exhibition.
☎ 01831 579478—Open April to October – involves walk
P Nearby **S** **£**

6 Broch of Midhowe

HY 372306 06 HS
Off B9064, SW of Island of Rousay, Orkney
Fine ruined broch and settlement, in a pleasant location by the sea. Midhowe chambered cairn nearby.
Open all year – short walk

7 Broch of Mousa

HU 457236 04 HS
Off A970, Island of Mousa, 14 miles S of Lerwick, off east coast, Shetland
The finest and most impressive surviving broch, standing to over 40 feet, and dating from the Iron Age.
Open all year – accessible by boat during good weather from Sandwick

8 Brown Caterthun

NO 555668 44 HS
Off A94, 4.5 miles N of Brechin, Angus
Large hill fort, dating from the Iron Age, with four ramparts and ditches.
Open all year – involves walk
P Nearby

9 Cairn Holy Chambered Cairns

NX 518540 83 HS
Off A75, 6.5 miles SE of Creetown, Dumfries & Galloway.
Two fine and relatively complete burial cairns, dating from Neolithic period.
Open all year
P

10 Cairnpapple Hill

NS 987717 65 HS
Off B792, 3 miles N of Bathgate, West Lothian
Stone circle and complex burial site, dating from about 3000 BC–1400 BC. Exhibition

13

Map 3: Ancient Sites – Orkney

PAPA WESTRAY
🏠 33/37
SANDAY
WESTRAY
43
ROUSAY
6 42
5 53
STRONSAY
4
MAINLAND
47
SHAPINSAY
44 51
Kirkwall
40 16 60
Stromness
26
HOY
SOUTH
RONALDSAY

and chamber containing early burials not accessible.

Open all year – involves short walk

11 Callanish Stones

NB 213330   08   HS

Off A858, 14 miles W of Stornoway, Lewis, Western Isles

A cross-shaped group of standing stones from about 3000 BC. Along with other circles in the complex, it is one of the most important and unique sites in Scotland. Visitor centre.

☎ 01851 621422—Open all year

P ☕ S ♿

12 Castlelaw

NT 229638   66   HS

Off A702, 2 miles W of Penicuik, Midlothian

Large Iron Age hill fort with ramparts and a souterrain, or earth house.

Open all year

13 Clava Cairns

NH 757445   27   HS

Off B9006 and B851, 7.5 miles E of Inverness, Highland

Two large and impressive chambered cairns and a ring cairn, dating from Neolithic period, surrounded by stone circles.

Open all year

P

14 Clickhimin Broch

HU 464408   04   HS

Off A970, 1 mile SW of Lerwick, Shetland

Well preserved and impressive broch, dating from Iron Age, with other buildings, including a block house.

Open all year

15 Corrimony Chambered Cairn

NH 383303   26   HS

Off A831, 8.5 miles W of Drumnadrochit, Glen Urquhart, Highland.

Fine chambered cairn, surrounded by a circle of standing stones.

Open all year

16 Cuween Hill Chambered Cairn

HY 364128   06   HS

Off A965, 7 miles NW of Kirkwall, 0.5 miles S of Finstown, Orkney

Chambered tomb, dating from the Neolithic period, with four chambers, once containing the remains of humans, dogs and oxen.

Open all year – involves short walk

P

17 Dere Street Roman Road

NT 452580   73   HS

On B6368, 10 miles S of Dalkeith, near Soutra Isle, Lothian

A length of road, called *Dere Street*.

Open all year

18 Dun Beag

NG 339385   32   HS

Off A863,1 mile W of Bracadale, Isle of Skye, Highland

Well preserved but ruined broch, with entrance passageway and mural stair.

Open all year

P

36 Kildalton Cross and Chapel

NR 458508 60 HS

*Off A846, 6.5 miles NE of Port Ellen, on
Islay*

The finest surviving High Cross in Scotland,
dating from the 9th century. Chapel and later
cross nearby.

Open all year

P Nearby

Kildalton Cross

37 Knap of Howar

NY 483519 05 HS

Island of Papa Westray, Orkney

Possibly the oldest standing stone house in
Europe, dating from the early Neolithic
period.

Open all year

38 Loanhead of Daviot Stone Circle

NJ 747288 38 HS

*Off A920, 5 miles NW of Inverurie,
Aberdeenshire*

Impressive recumbent stone circle, dating
from about 4500 BC, with a small burial
enclosure.

Open all year

P

39 Machrie Moor Stone Circles

NR 910324 69 HS

*Off A841, 3 miles N of Blackwaterfoot,
Arran*

The remains of six stone circles, some dating
from the Bronze Age, one of the most
important sites of its type in Scotland.

Open all year – 1.5 mile walk

40 Maes Howe

HY 318128 06 HS

On A965, 9 miles W of Kirkwall, Orkney

The finest tomb in the British Isles, dating
from the Neolithic period. A large mound
covers a stone passage and burial chamber
with three cells.

☎ 01856 761606—Open all year

P ☕ S WC ♿

41 Meigle Sculptured Stone Museum

NO 287447 53 HS

On A94, Meigle, Angus

A collection of 25 sculpted stones, one of the
best collections of Dark Age sculpture in
Western Europe.

☎ 01828 640612—Open April to
September

WC ♿

42 Midhowe Chambered Cairn

HY 373306 06 HS

Off B9064, Island of Rousay, Orkney.

Large chambered tomb, with 24 stalls, which
dates from the Neolithic period. Protected
by a modern building. Near to Broch of
Midhowe.

Open all year

43 Quoyness Chambered Cairn

HY 677378 05 HS

Island of Sanday, Orkney

Chambered tomb, dating from the Neolithic
period, containing a passage and main
chamber with six cells.

Open all year

44 Ring of Brodgar Circle
HY 294134   06   HS
On B9055, 5 miles NE of Stromness,
Orkney
Most impressive stone circle in Scotland,
consisting of a large circle enclosed by a
ditch with two causeways. Dates from about
3000 BC.
Open all year
P

45 Rough Castle
NS 835798–NS 845799   65   HS
Off B816, 1.5 miles E of Bonnybridge, nr
Falkirk
Length of Roman rampart and ditch of the
Antonine Wall, together with the earthworks
of a fort.
Open all year

46 Ruthwell Cross
NY 100682   85   HS
Off B724, 8.5 miles SE of Dumfries, at
Ruthwell
An Anglian sculpted cross, dating from the
7th century.
Open all year – sited within the Parish
church, key available from nearby
house.
P

47 Skara Brae
HY 231188   06   HS
Off B9056, 7 miles N of Stromness, Orkney
Best preserved group of ancient houses in
Europe, dating from the Neolithic period.
The houses contain stone furniture, hearths
and drains.
☎ 01856 841815—Open all year –
involves short walk
P **S** &

48 St Andrews Cathedral
NO 516166   59   HS
Off A91, St Andrews, Fife
The very ruined remains of the largest
cathedral in Scotland, with St Rule's Tower.
Museum houses a fine collection of early

Christian and medieval sculpture. The castle
is nearby.
☎ 01334 472563—Open all year
P Nearby **S** &

49 St Ninian's Cave
NX 421359   83   HS
Off A747, 4 miles SW of Whithorn, at
Physgill, on coast
Associated with Saint Ninian, crosses are
carved on the walls of this cave.
Open all year – involves walk
P

50 St Vigeans Sculpted Stones
NO 637430   54   HS
Off A933, St Vigeans village, 0.5 miles N of
Arbroath
Fine collection of early Christian and Pictish
stones housed in cottages. Exhibition.
Open April to September – interesting
church of St Vigeans nearby
P Nearby

51 Stones of Steness
HY 306126   06   HS
On B9055, 5 miles NE of Stromness, Orkney
Remains of a stone circle, dating from the
Neolithic period, surrounded by a ditch.
Open all year
P

52 Sueno's Stone
NJ 046595   27   HS
Off A96, E side of Forres, Moray
The most remarkable sculpted stone in
Scotland, dating from about 900 AD.
Open all year – protected (and
obscured) by glass enclosure
P

53 Taversöe Tuick Chambered Cairn
HY 426276   06   HS
On B9065, Island of Rousay, Orkney
Chambered tomb, dating from the Neolithic
period, with two burial chambers, one above
the other.
Open all year

54 Temple Wood Stone Circles

NR 826978 55 HS
Off A816, 1 mile S of Kilmartin, Argyll
Amongst a cluster of cairns and other prehistoric monuments, a circle of upright stones, and the remains of anearlier circle, dating from about 3000 BC.
Open all year

55 The Chesters

NT 507782 66 HS
Off B1377 or B1343, 1 mile south of Drem, East Lothian
Iron Age hill fort, with elaborate system of ramparts and ditches.
Open all year

56 Tomnaverie Stone Circle

NJ 486034 37 HS
On B9094, 3.5 miles NW of Aboyne, Aberdeenshire
Recumbent stone circle, dating from about 4000 BC. Good views.
Open all year

57 Torhouse Stone Circle

NX 382565 83 HS
Off B733, 3.5 miles W of Wigtown, Dumfries and Galloway
Unusual recumbent stone circle, with 19 boulders, dating from Bronze Age.
Open all year

58 White Caterthun

NO 547660 44 HS
Off A94, 4 miles N of Brechin, Angus
Large hill fort, dating from the Iron Age, with massive stone rampart, ditch and outer ramparts
Open all year

59 Whithorn Priory

NX 444403 83 HS
On A746 in Whithorn, Dumfries & Galloway
Site of 5th-century community of St Ninian, although the ruins are of a 12th-century

Whithorn Priory

priory. Fine collection of early Christian sculpture in nearby museum.
☎ 01988 500508—Open March to October
🅿 Nearby ♿

60 Wideford Hill Chambered Cairn

HY 409122 06 HS
Off A965, 2 miles W of Kirkwall, Orkney
Interesting chambered cairn, dating from the Neolithic period, with three cells.
Open all year – involves long walk

Map 4: Sons of Canmore

SHETLAND

•Lerwick

ORKNEY

•Kirkwall

Bishop's Palace

Thurso•

CAITHNESS

SUTHERLAND

•**Wick**

LEWIS

Stornoway

HARRIS

NORTH UIST

SOUTH UIST

SKYE

BARRA

•Ullapool

•Kinloss •Elgin

Fraserburgh

Inverness•

MORAY

Aberdeen•

•**Fort William**

MULL

Iona

•Dunstaffnage
•**Oban**

ARGYLL

JURA

Tarbert•

ISLAY

Perth• •Scone

Dundee

•Arbroath

Montrose

•St Andrews

Stirling • Dunfermline• •Kinghorn
•Dumbarton •Inchcolm
•Edinburgh •Dunbar

Bothwell

•**Lanark**

Largs
(1263)

BUTE

•**Ayr**

ARRAN

Melrose•• •Kelso
Dryburgh •Jedburgh

Berwick

NORTHUMBERLAND

•Dumfries

ENGLAND

GALLOWAY

Stranraer• Wigtown•

•Kirkcudbright

20

PART TWO: THE MIDDLE AGES

Sons of Canmore

1066 Battle of Hastings

After William the Conqueror's defeat of King Harold and the English, at Hastings in the south of England, many Anglo-Saxons settled in the south of Scotland at Malcolm Canmore's invitation. Although Scotland was never conquered as England had been, the coming of the Normans had as profound an effect, reducing the Celtic influence, but strengthening the nation for the wars with the English in following centuries.

1068 Marriage of Malcolm Canmore to Margaret

In 1068 Malcolm Canmore married Margaret, sister of the Saxon heir to the throne of England, who had fled to Scotland with her brother. The marriage greatly angered William the Conqueror. Malcolm's first wife, Ingibiorg, by whom he had had several children including a son Duncan, had recently died.

Margaret, whose chapel survives in Edinburgh Castle, preferred English ways to those of her Celtic subjects. Her sons were given English names, she practised European customs and culture at court, she encouraged monastic foundations, such as that at Dunfermline, of which the church still survives, and revived the monastery on Iona. This led to discontent amongst some of Malcolm's subjects. Margaret, however, appears to have been a very pious woman, doing good works – according to her devoted biographer Turgot – and was later made a saint.

Dunfermline Abbey

1072 William the Conqueror invades Scotland

Malcolm Canmore attacked England and ravaged Northumberland. William the

21

Conqueror, angered by the attack and Malcolm's marriage, invaded Scotland in 1072, forcing Canmore to pay homage to him. Malcolm responded with further raids into England, but in 1093 was treacherously murdered when accepting the surrender of Alnwick Castle, in Northumberland. Margaret died soon afterwards, at Edinburgh Castle, and she and Malcolm were buried in Dunfermline Abbey. Scotland was again plunged into dynastic turmoil.

1093 Donald Bane (Donald III), Duncan II & Edmund

Donald III, Donald Bane – Bane meaning *fair* – the 60-year-old brother of Malcolm Canmore, siezed the throne and drove out Margaret's sons, partly because many resented the growing influence of the English and Normans. Donald was overthrown in turn in 1094 by Duncan II – Malcolm Canmore's eldest son by his first wife Ingibiorg – with English help. However, Duncan was not popular and was murdered. Donald III recovered the throne, this time aided by Edmund, son of Malcolm and Margaret. Edgar, another of their sons, defeated Donald and Edmund, again with an English army. Donald was blinded and was imprisoned on Iona, while Edmund retired to a monastery in England.

1097–1107 Edgar the Peaceable & Alexander the Fierce

A time of relative peace, Edgar the Peaceable ruled Scotland well, although he ceded the Western Isles to the Norwegians, including Iona. Edgar did not marry and his brother, Alexander, succeeded him. Alexander earned his nickname *The Fierce* by savagely putting down a rising in Moray. However, he encouraged monastic settlements in Scotland, and founded Inchcolm Abbey, which is now an impressive ruin. He married Sibylla, an illegitimate daughter of Henry I of England. This match does not appear to have been happy, and Alexander died in 1124 without a son or daughter.

Kelso Abbey (see next page)

1124 David I

David I, brother of Alexander, came to the throne. He was married to Matilda, an English heiress, and David acquired the wealthy Earldom of Huntingdon in England, as well as other lands. He had spent many years in exile in England, and during this time had become friendly with many Norman families. He invited some of these men, with names such as Bruce, Comyn, and FitzAllan (Stewarts) to Scotland, and gave them land or married them to heiresses.

David also mostly ruled well, and burghs, with special trading privileges, were introduced. He founded abbeys at Holyrood, Edinburgh; Melrose; Dryburgh; Kelso; Newbattle, near Edinburgh; Kinloss; and Jedburgh. Melrose Abbey is a substantial ruin, as are Jedburgh and Dryburgh, while Holyrood Palace is built near the ruins of the old Abbey church. This increased the prosperity of the nation by encouraging trade and improving agriculture, although David had to put down rebellions in Moray in 1130, and in 1140.

Holyrood Abbey

1138 Battle of the Standard

David became involved in the fighting in England between Stephen of Blois and his niece, the rightful heir, Maud or Matilda. He invaded England on her behalf, but at the Battle of the Standard, near Northallerton, the Scots suffered a crushing defeat. However, David managed to acquire Northumberland and Cumberland in 1139 from the English when they were in disarray. The kingdom of Scots reached its furthest extent southwards. David died in 1153 at his prayers at Carlisle Castle.

1153 Malcolm the Maiden

Malcolm the Maiden, David's grandson, came to the throne in 1153 when he was 11 years old. He was called *the Maiden* because he took a vow of celibacy and never married. Malcolm lost the Earldom of Northumberland, exchanging it for the Earldom of Huntingdon with Henry II of England. He put down risings in 1160 by Fergus, Earl of Galloway, in the south-west, as well as by Somerled.

Somerled had pushed the Norsemen out of much of the Hebrides between 1156-8, making himself an independent prince. He was assassinated at Renfrew before a battle with Malcolm's forces. Somerled's sons divided his lands, and it was from him that the MacDonalds and MacDougalls originated.

Malcolm the Maiden died at the age of 23 without children.

1174–1214 William the Lyon

William the Lyon, brother of Malcolm, became King of Scots in 1174. After putting down a rebellion in Galloway, William tried to recover Northumberland in 1175 and invaded the north of England. He was captured by the English at Alnwick, and was held at Falaise in Normandy until he swore fealty to Henry II of England as his overlord.

In 1176 William had the abbey at Arbroath built, in memory of his friend, Thomas à Becket, who had been murdered in 1168. He brought the north of Scotland under his control during campaigns in 1179 and 1187, finally taking Caithness and Sutherland from Harald Maddadson, Earl of Orkney, who was blinded and castrated.

William restored Scotland's independence in 1189 by paying Richard the Lionheart 10 000 merks. During his reign the Scottish church was recognised by the Pope as being separate from that of the English.

He was married in 1186 to Ermengarde de Beaumont, and they had a son, Alexander, as well as three daughters. William died in 1214.

The lion rampant was used as a heraldic device by Scottish kings, and may have been introduced by William. It is still used on the Scottish Standard by the current monarch.

1214–49 Alexander II

Alexander II, son of William the Lyon, came to the throne in 1214. Again he had to put down rebellions in Argyll, Caithness and Galloway, building castles at Tarbert, Dunstaffnage – which is an impressive ruin – Kirkcudbright and Wigtown. Alexander was known as a law-maker, and a collection of laws, called *Regiam Majestatem*, was compiled at this time. Alexander tried to recover the Hebrides from Norway, but died at Kerrera, an island near Oban, and was succeeded by his young son, Alexander III.

1249–86 Alexander III

Alexander III, then only eight, came to the throne, and was married to Margaret, the 11-year-old daughter of Henry II, King of England, in 1251. Alexander managed to keep peace with England, and the nation prospered during his long reign. He further strengthened the mechanisms of government and justice, and built many royal castles to enforce his authority throughout the kingdom.

1263 Battle of Largs & Treaty of Perth

Alexander III attacked the island of Skye in an attempt to wrest the Hebrides from Haco, King of Norway. Haco responded by raising a large army and sailing south in an armada of long ships. A storm wrecked many of the ships, and a reduced force of Norwegians was engaged at the Battle of Largs. Haco and his army retreated, and he died at the Bishop's Palace, in Kirkwall on Orkney. The Bishop's

Bishop's Palace, Kirkwall

Palace is an interesting ruin and stands beside the Earl's Palace and St Magnus Cathedral. In 1266 at the Treaty of Perth, Magnus IV of Norway ceded the Hebrides and the Isle of Man to the Scots.

1286 Death of Alexander III

Margaret, Alexander's wife, died in 1275, and their elder son in 1284. Alexander had no other children, and in 1285 married the young and beautiful Yolande de Dreux. On a stormy night on his way to meet her, hoping to give her an heir, he fell to his death off the cliffs at Kinghorn – the spot marked by a monument – and plunged Scotland into a war that nearly saw the country and its people absorbed into England.

> When Alexander our king wis deid
> That Scotland led in lauche and le[1]
> Away was sonse[2] of ale and breid
> Of wine and wax, of gamin and glee
> Our gold was changit into leid
> The fruit failet on every tree
> Christ succour Scotland and remeid
> That stade[3] us in perplexitie
>
> *Anonymous*

[1] law and peace [2] plenty [3] beset

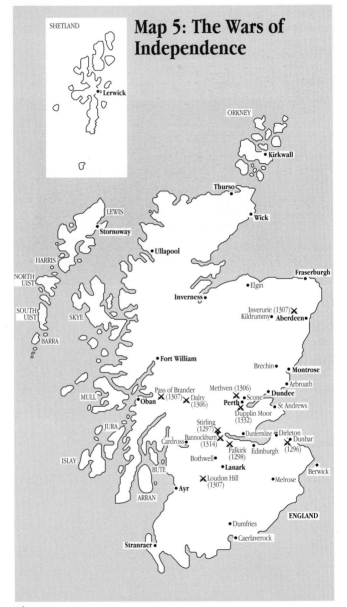

SHETLAND

•⊷Lerwick

Map 5: The Wars of Independence

ORKNEY

•Kirkwall

Thurso

Wick

LEWIS

Stornoway

HARRIS

NORTH
UIST

Ullapool

SOUTH
UIST

SKYE

Inverness•

Elgin

Fraserburgh

BARRA

Inverurie (1307) ✕
Kildrummy• Aberdeen•

• Fort William

Brechin •

Montrose

MULL

Pass of Brander
(1307)
✕
• Oban

Methven (1306)
✕
Dalry
(1306)
Perth•

Scone
•
•Dundee
Arbroath

•St Andrews

JURA

Stirling
(1297)
✕
Cardross•

Bannockburn
✕
(1314)

Dupplin Moor
(1332)

•Dunfermline

Dirleton

•Dunbar
(1296)

ISLAY

BUTE

Bothwell•

Falkirk
(1298)

Edinburgh

•Lanark

✕Loudon Hill
(1307)

Berwick

•Melrose

•Ayr

ARRAN

ENGLAND

•Dumfries

Stranraer•

•Caerlaverock

The Wars of Independence

1289 Margaret, the Maid of Norway

Margaret, the Maid of Norway, was the next in line to the throne. She was the daughter of Margaret – daughter of Alexander II, who had died in 1283 – and the King of Norway.

It was agreed that Margaret, the Maid of Norway, should be brought to Scotland from Norway, and in the meantime the kingdom was to be ruled by six Guardians. In an attempt to avoid civil war, they asked Edward I of England – who had been friendly to the Scots – to help them. At the Treaty of Birgham, a marriage was arranged between Margaret and the son of Edward I of England, although this treaty stated that homage should not be paid to an English monarch, and all Scottish institutions should remain independent.

1290–96 Death of Maid of Norway & Balliol becomes King

On her way to Scotland, Margaret died, reportedly from sea sickness, having only got as far as Orkney.

One of the Guardians, Bishop Fraser, fearing civil war, then unwisely asked Edward I of England to choose a king from 13 claimants, including John Balliol and Robert Bruce, the grandfather of the future king. Edward summoned the claimants to Norham Castle – now a substantial ruin in Northumberland – first getting them to swear allegiance to him. Edward then chose John Balliol, who accepted the English king as his overlord, Superior and Lord Paramount of Scotland.

1295 Treaty with France: the *Auld Alliance*

John Balliol married Isabel de Warenne, and they had a son, Edward.

Balliol tried to restore royal authority, but was hampered by the interference of Edward of England, and the Bruces, who still had designs on the throne themselves. Edward I of England tried to provoke Balliol into defiance, and when in 1295 the Scots signed a treaty with France, England's enemy, so beginning the *Auld Alliance*, Edward had the excuse he needed to crush the Scots once and for all.

1296 Edward I invades Scotland & the Battle of Dunbar

Balliol's resistance against Edward I only stung the English king to act. An English army, said to number 35 000 men, invaded Scotland, and sacked Berwick – then a rich Scottish burgh – slaughtering 16 000 of its inhabitants: men, women and children.

A large but inexperienced Scottish army was heavily defeated by Edward at the Battle of Dunbar, and the English occupied much of Scotland, advancing all the way to Elgin. Balliol surrendered at Brechin, earning his nickname *Toom Tabard* – empty coat – and was stripped of his office.

Edward took over control of Scotland, installing English garrisons in many castles. He eventually returned to the south, taking with him the Stone of

Destiny and Coronation Chair, on which the kings of Scots had been inaugurated, and many other treasures.

The Stone of Destiny was kept beneath the Coronation Chair in Westminster Abbey in England, but is to be returned, to Edinburgh Castle, after 700 years. Scone Palace stands on the site of the abbey from which the stone was taken.

Edward forced over 2 000 nobles, churchmen and landholders to swear allegiance to him. The list of their names became known as *The Ragman Roll*, after the ragged look of all the different seals and ribbons.

1297–1305 William Wallace: Battles of Stirling Bridge & Falkirk

The English occupation was harsh and the Scots rose, led by William Wallace and Sir Andrew Moray. Wallace was a son of the laird of Elderslie, and his wife had probably been murdered by the English sheriff of Lanark. Wallace was a successful guerrilla leader, and was greatly admired by the general population, although much of the nobility viewed him with suspicion. This included the Bruces, who still wished to assert their own claim to the throne – Wallace supported Balliol.

In 1297 Wallace and Moray defeated a large English army at Stirling Bridge, where Hugh de Cressingham, Edward's treasurer of Scotland, was skinned and turned into a saddle bag. Moray died soon afterwards, possibly from wounds received at the battle.

Wallace was knighted and became a Guardian, and ravaged the north of England. This prompted Edward into invading Scotland in 1298, and he crushed any Scottish resistance by defeating Wallace at the Battle of Falkirk. Many nobles fled the battle rather than fight on with Wallace.

Wallace left Scotland on a diplomatic mission to the continent, but when he returned was betrayed and captured by the English, then hanged, drawn and quartered in London in 1305. In killing Wallace so horribly, Edward I had only succeeded in creating a national hero.

1305–08 Robert the Bruce & the Wars of Independence

Robert the Bruce had a claim to the throne as a descendant of David, Earl of Huntingdon, brother of both William the Lyon and Malcolm the Maiden. Bruce was first married to Isabella of Mar, and it was through their daughter Marjorie that the Stewarts became kings. By his second wife, Elizabeth de Burgh, he had a son, David.

In 1306 Bruce agreed to meet John Comyn of Badenoch, who had a more direct claim to the throne, and was related to John Balliol. The Comyns were one of the most powerful families in Scotland, supported by the MacDougalls of Lorne, MacDowalls of Galloway, and Earl of Ross.

Bruce and Comyn met in a church at Dumfries to resolve their differences, but the two men argued and Comyn was stabbed to death by Bruce. Although Bruce was a hunted fugitive, and was excommunicated, he declared himself King of Scots at Scone in 1306. His small army was defeated at Methven, and then scattered at Dalry, and he had to flee the country. He lost more than these battles: three of his brothers, Nigel, Thomas and Alexander, were executed by the English; his sister, Mary, was hung from a cage at Roxburgh Castle; his sister and daughter Christine and Marjorie, along with his second wife, Elizabeth de Burgh, were imprisoned.

Luckily for Bruce, however, Edward I of England died in July 1307 at Burgh by Sands, just on the English side of the Border. Edward died berating his son to ravage Scotland, but Edward II was not as ruthless or effective, and retreated to bury his father.

Bruce returned to Scotland and won battles at Loudoun Hill; the Pass of Brander, where he defeated the MacDougalls; in Galloway, where the MacDowalls were crushed; and at Inverurie, where he destroyed the power of the Comyns, and their allies, and wasted Buchan. The Earl of Ross submitted to Bruce. Other risings expelled the English garrisons from most Scottish castles, until only Stirling Castle was in the hands of the English. James Douglas, Neil Campbell, Angus Og MacDonald, and the High Stewards or Stewarts were among Bruce's loyal supporters, all important families in the later history of Scotland.

It was Bruce's policy to destroy castles so that they could not be held by the English. However, Bothwell, Dirleton, Caerlaverock and Kildrummy castles all

Caerlaverock Castle

survive – in part – from before the Wars of Independence.

1314 Battle of Bannockburn

By 1314, only Stirling Castle – on its rock and still a vast fortress – was held by the English, and was besieged by the Scots. Edward II and a large army marched north to relieve the castle. On the eve of the battle, Henry de Bohun challenged Bruce to single combat, but Bruce clove de Bohun's head with an axe. Although outnumbered three to one, the Scots won the Battle of Bannockburn, and many of the English were slaughtered or captured, although this was as much due to their bad tactics and poor leadership. The battle site is open to the public.

1320 Declaration of Arbroath

Battles continued and although the Scots had the best of it, notably by defeating the English deep into England at the Battle of Byland, Edward II would not recognise Scotland's independence – nor would the Pope. A Declaration, sealed by most of the nobles of Scotland, was drawn up at Arbroath Abbey, which urged the Pope to recognise Scotland as a free independent country, and to put pressure on the English to do the same.

Bothwell Castle (see previous page)

1329 Death of Robert the Bruce & Accession of David II

Edward III finally recognised Scotland's independence in 1328, the year before Bruce died, reportedly from leprosy, at Cardross, near Dumbarton. Bruce's heart was removed from his body, and taken on a crusade to Granada by James Douglas, although it was eventually interred at Melrose Abbey. A lead casket was recently excavated from the Abbey, and is believed to contain Bruce's heart. This

Melrose Abbey

act is commemorated by the heart on the Douglas coat of arms. The rest of Bruce's body was buried at Dunfermline. David, his young son, was made king, but peace lasted for only a few years after Bruce's death.

1332–41 Edward Balliol & the Battle of Halidon Hill

Edward, son of John Balliol, invaded Scotland, with help from Edward III and the English, and was made king after defeating a Scottish army at Dupplin Moor. David II was sent to France for safety.

Edward III of England was a much more able king than Edward II, and besieged Berwick, crushing a Scottish army at the Battle of Halidon Hill, near Berwick, in 1333. Although Edward Balliol was initially successful, he was eventually defeated by Andrew Moray the Regent, son of the victor of the Battle of Stirling Bridge, and had to flee Scotland in 1341.

1346–71 Battle of Neville's Cross & the Treaty of Berwick

David II returned to Scotland, and led an invasion of England in support of the French, who were at war with the English – this was not the only time that the *Auld Alliance* would harm the Scots. The Scots were heavily defeated by the English at the Battle of Neville's Cross in the north of England, and David was taken prisoner. David fought bravely, but in vain, although Robert the High Steward fled the battle.

Edward ravaged the south of Scotland in 1356, known as the *Burnt Candlemas*. However, in 1357 David was released after a ransom of 100 000 merks was agreed, although the Scots never paid most of the money.

David died in 1371 at Edinburgh Castle, without heir, although he was twice married: to Joan of England, who died in 1362; and to a former mistress, Margaret Logie. Although he hated the Stewarts, partly because of the cowardly action of Robert the High Steward, he could not prevent the succession to the throne of Robert II, son of Marjorie – daughter of Robert the Bruce – and Walter the High Steward. David reportedly would have offered the English king the throne if he had been allowed. The Stewarts were so named because they were the High Stewards of the kingdom, their original family name having been FitzAllan.

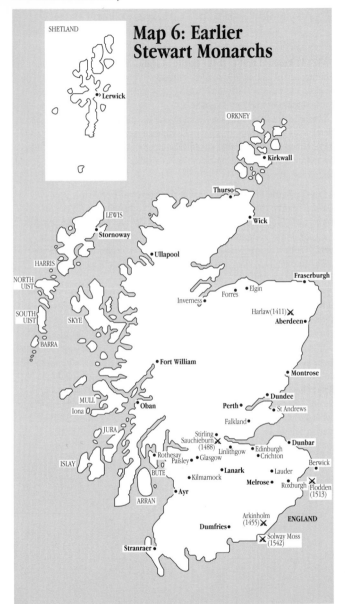

SHETLAND

•› Lerwick

Map 6: Earlier Stewart Monarchs

ORKNEY

• Kirkwall

Thurso •

• Wick

LEWIS

• Stornoway

• Ullapool

HARRIS

NORTH UIST

Fraserburgh •

Inverness •   Forres   • Elgin

SOUTH UIST

SKYE

Harlaw(1411) ✕

Aberdeen •

BARRA

• Fort William

• Montrose

MULL

• Oban   Perth •   • Dundee

Iona 0   St Andrews

JURA   Falkland •

Stirling •

Sauchieburn ✕   • Dunbar

(1488)   Linlithgow

ISLAY   Rothesay •   • Edinburgh

Paisley • Glasgow • Crichton   Berwick •

BUTE   • Lanark   • Lauder

• Kilmarnock   Melrose •   Roxburgh • ✕ Flodden

ARRAN   • Ayr   (1513)

Arkinholm   ENGLAND

(1455) ✕

Dumfries •   ✕ Solway Moss

(1542)

Stranraer •

Earlier Stewart Monarchs

1371–88 Robert II

Robert II came to the throne when already 55 years of age, although as Guardian of the Realm, he had been involved in defending the country against the English. He became increasingly infirm, and control of the kingdom passed to his eldest son, John, Earl of Carrick; and then to his next son, Robert, later Duke of Albany. Robert II was married to Elizabeth Mure, and then to Euphemia Ross, by whom he had many children.

1388–90 The Battle of Otterburn & Death of Robert II

Fighting between England and Scotland continued. The English, under the Percy Earl of Northumberland, raided as far as Edinburgh in 1383, and again in 1385, although it was meant to be a time of truce.

The Scots got their revenge at the Battle of Otterburn in 1388, where they defeated a force led by Percy and captured him, although the Earl of Douglas, leader of the Scottish army, was killed at the battle.

In 1390 Robert II died at Dundonald Castle and was succeeded by his son, John. However, the name *John* was not seen as a suitable name for a king of Scots, and he was crowned as Robert III.

1390-1406 Robert III & the Battle of Homildon Hill

Robert III had been left lame by a kick from a horse, and did not have the ruthlessness or vigour to rule well. He said of himself that his epitaph should be *Here lies the worst of kings and the most miserable of men*. During this time, the power of the MacDonald Lord of the Isles increased until they ruled a virtually independent kingdom in the north and west; in the Borders, the Douglas family was supremely powerful.

One brother of Robert III, Alexander Stewart, the Wolf of Badenoch, made himself Earl of Buchan by forcing the Countess of Buchan to marry him. When he was excommunicated by the Bishop of Moray, he sacked the town of Forres, and torched the town and cathedral of Elgin.

The kingdom was increasingly ruled by another brother, Robert, Duke of Albany. Robert III had a son, David, Duke of Rothesay, by his wife Anabella Drummond, as well as many other children. Uncle and nephew, Albany and David, Duke of Rothesay, competed with each other for power, until Albany had David imprisoned, and probably starved to death, at Falkland Palace in 1402.

The Scots raided deep into England the same year – but on their return, laden with plunder, were heavily defeated by the English, led by the Percys, at Homildon Hill, near Wooler, in Northumberland. The Earl of Douglas, leader of the army, was among those captured.

Partly to remove him from any possible harm from his uncle Albany, the young James, son of Robert III, and now heir to the throne, was sent to France. On his journey, however, he was captured by the English and imprisoned by Henry IV.

Robert III died at Rothesay Castle in 1406, a few days after hearing of his son's fate, and – there being none to oppose him, with James, the heir to the throne, imprisoned in the Tower of London – Albany ruled the kingdom. He may even have tipped off the English that James was being sent to France.

1410 Founding of St Andrews University

Teaching began at St Andrews in this year, and was formalised in 1413.

1411 The Battle of Harlaw

In pursuing his claim to the Earldom of Ross, Donald MacDonald, Lord of the Isles, descendant of Somerled, invaded the mainland of Scotland and marched on Aberdeen. He was met by an army, led by Alexander Stewart, illegitimate son of the Wolf of Badenoch, who had made himself Earl of Mar by forcing the Countess of Mar to marry him – like father, like son. The MacDonald forces were defeated and retreated, although with such slaughter on both sides the battle is known as the *Red Harlaw*.

1424–37 James I

James I was released from imprisonment in England, after a ransom was paid by the Scots. During his captivity, he was married to Joan Beaufort, and they had a son James, born in 1430, as well as other children.

Although Albany was already dead, James had Murdoch, his son, executed. However, James did not rule well, making himself unpopular by his uneven enforcement of order and high-handedness towards the nobles. In 1427 he imprisoned Donald, Lord of the Isles, and many other Highland chiefs, and had some of them executed – stinging Donald into ravaging Inverness and Lochaber.

James was murdered at Perth in 1437 by a party of disgruntled nobles. Joan, his wife, had the murderers captured and cruelly tortured before execution. James's heart was taken on a pilgrimage to the East, and later brought back from Rhodes by a Knight of St John.

Crichton Castle (see next page)

1437–60 James II & the Destruction of the Black Douglases

James II, son of James I, came to the throne when he was only six. James had a red birth-mark covering half of his face, which gave him his nickname *James of the Fiery Face*.

The families of Crichton and Livingston competed for power during his minority. They united briefly to murder the 6th Earl of Douglas, at the *Black Dinner* at Edinburgh Castle in 1440, as they both feared the power of the Douglases. Not unreasonably, the Douglases besieged Edinburgh Castle, and sacked Crichton Castle – now a fine ruin – although the 7th Earl of Douglas, James the Gross, may have had a hand in the murder.

James II married Mary of Gueldres in 1449, when he finally assumed power, and they had a son, another James, in 1452. James II encouraged the arts and science, and Glasgow University was founded in 1450.

The Black Douglas family were very powerful in Scotland during his reign, having acquired much land and power through James Douglas, a supporter and friend of Robert the Bruce. The Douglases were allied with the Lindsay Earls of Crawford and the MacDonald Lord of the Isles.

James II, fearing this alliance and detesting their pride, murdered William, 8th Earl of Douglas in Stirling Castle, despite having promised him safe conduct. James took, and destroyed, many Douglas strongholds, including the castle of Threave, and the Black Douglases were finally defeated and their power destroyed at the Battle of Arkinholm in 1455. James II then attempted to recover Roxburgh Castle and the town of Berwick from the English, but was killed by an exploding cannon at Roxburgh in 1460, at the age of 29. He was buried in Holyrood Abbey.

1460–88 James III & the Battle of Sauchieburn

James III was only eight when he became king, and during his minority the Boyd Earls of Kilmarnock were very powerful, having siezed and imprisoned the young king.

James III married Margaret of Denmark in 1469, and so acquired Orkney and Shetland as part of the dowry. They had a son, another James.

James III destroyed the power of the Boyds in retaliation for their earlier behaviour, but made himself very unpopular by acquiring much of the lands and property of the nobility. In 1482 the King's favourite, Cochrane, and other friends of the king, were hanged by Archibald *Bell the Cat* Douglas, Earl of Angus, from Lauder Bridge in front of the king. In 1482 and 1484 disgruntled nobles, such as the 9th Earl of Douglas, helped the English raid Scotland.

The Scottish nobles eventually decided to replace James with his 15-year-old son, the future James IV. James III raised an army, but was defeated at the Battle of Sauchieburn in 1488, and reputedly murdered after the battle by an assassin disguised as a priest. He was buried in Cambuskenneth Abbey, near Stirling.

The first recorded use of the thistle was in 1470, when it embellished one side of coins minted in Edinburgh.

1488–1513 James IV & the Battle of Flodden

James IV came to the throne when he was 15, and took control of the kingdom, although he reputedly wore a heavy iron chain for the rest of his life in penance for the death of his father. He ruled well, extending civil and criminal justice.

James destroyed the power of the Lord of the Isles in a campaign to the Hebrides in 1493, the final Lord of the Isles ending his days in Paisley Abbey.

James signed a treaty of *perpetual peace* with England at his marriage in 1502 to Margaret Tudor, sister of Henry VIII of England, although the couple do not seem to have liked each other. Enough, however, to have a son, James, born in 1512.

He encouraged science and literature, and in 1507 printing was introduced to Scotland. He also remodelled the palaces at Linlithgow, Falkland and Holyrood; and he had the *Great Michael*, a huge warship, built at Newhaven, near Edinburgh. Aberdeen University was founded, and whisky was drunk in the court by the end of his reign.

However, the English and French went to war, and in 1513, in support of France, James IV invaded England, although a peace had already been signed. At the Battle of Flodden, in Northumberland, despite holding a strong position, the Scottish army was disastrously defeated. James IV was slain, as were many Scottish nobles, lords, churchmen and soldiers, the worst defeat a Scottish army was ever to suffer.

Linlithgow Palace

1513–42 James V & the Battle of Solway Moss

James V was only one year old when he came to the throne. Margaret Tudor, widow of James IV, married the Douglas Earl of Angus, and the young king was kept a prisoner by Angus between 1526–8. Angus supported the English, but James wanted a French marriage, and eventually married Mary of Guise, by whom he had a daughter, Mary, in 1542 – after his first wife, Madeleine of France, had died. James also patronised the arts, and remodelled Stirling Castle. He, too, hated the Douglas family with a passion until he died – even pursuing his vendetta to Janet Douglas, Lady Glamis, whom he had burnt to death for witchcraft in 1537.

James made himself unpopular by his acquisitiveness from wealthy subjects and his reliance on disliked favourites. He enforced rule of law on the Border by dealing harshly with reivers such as the Armstrongs, further alienating many families. He decided to invade England in 1542, but his army was divided by dislike of both James and his general and favourite, Oliver Sinclair. The Scottish army was soundly defeated by the English at the Battle of Solway Moss.

James died at Falkland Palace shortly after the battle, hearing of the birth of his daughter by Mary of Guise, at Linlithgow Palace. He reportedly said on his death bed *It cam wi' a lass and it'll gang wi' a lass*, meaning that the Stewarts had gained the throne through Marjorie Bruce and would lose it through his daughter, Mary, later Queen of Scots. He was wrong, however, as Mary married her cousin, Henry

Falkland Palace

Stewart, Lord Darnley, from a close branch of the family.

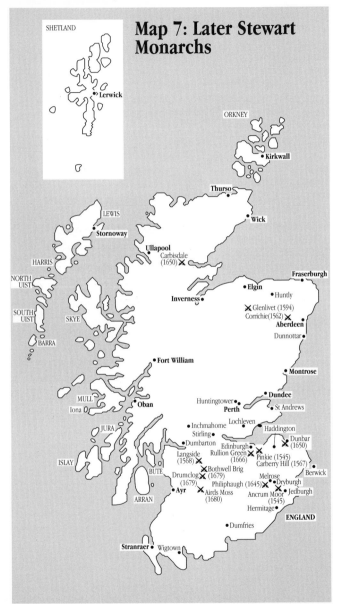

Map 7: Later Stewart Monarchs

SHETLAND

• Lerwick

ORKNEY

• Kirkwall

Thurso

• Wick

LEWIS

• Stornoway

HARRIS

Ullapool •
Carbisdale
(1650) ✕

Fraserburgh

NORTH
UIST

SOUTH
UIST

SKYE

• Elgin
• Huntly

Inverness •

✕ Glenlivet (1594)
Corrichie (1562) ✕
Aberdeen

BARRA

Dunnottar

• Fort William

Montrose

MULL

• Oban

Iona

JURA

Huntingtower •
Perth •

• Dundee
St Andrews

• Inchmahome
Stirling •
Lochleven •

Haddington

• Dumbarton
Langside (1568) ✕

Edinburgh • Rullion Green ✕
(1666)

• Dunbar
(1650)

Pinkie (1545)
Carberry Hill (1567) ✕

ISLAY

BUTE

Drumclog ✕
(1679)

✕ Bothwell Brig (1679)

Melrose •
Philiphaugh (1645) ✕ • Dryburgh

Berwick

ARRAN

• Ayr

✕ Airds Moss
(1680)

Ancrum Moor
(1545)

Jedburgh •

Hermitage •

ENGLAND

• Dumfries

Stranraer • Wigtown

Later Stewart Monarchs

1544–50 *The Rough Wooing* & Hertford's Invasions

Struggles followed the death of James: between Mary of Guise, who supported the French, and the Hamilton Earl of Arran, Governor until 1554, who supported the English.

A treaty had been signed with the English that Mary, Queen of Scots, was to marry Edward, son of Henry VIII – but the Scots broke the agreement. In revenge, the south-east of Scotland was ravaged by the English, including the sacking of the abbeys at Melrose, Jedburgh, Dryburgh and Holyrood; castles; and villages – 243 in all – by the Earl of Hertford. This became known as the *Rough Wooing*, a less than gentle attempt to encourage the Scots to change their mind.

A small English army was slaughtered at the Battle of Ancrum Moor in 1545, but the English invaded again and in 1547 the Scots, led by Hamilton, were heavily defeated at the Battle of Pinkie. Much of southern Scotland was held by the English, who built a series of forts, including those at Haddington; Dunglass, south of Dunbar; and Eyemouth, north of Berwick.

The young Mary, Queen of Scots, who had been lodged at Inchmahome Priory and Dumbarton Castle, was sent to France for safety in 1548. By 1550, however, the Scots, with French help, had fought back. The English were forced to retreat from most of Scotland, abandoning the fort at Haddington after a long siege.

1550–8 The Reformation

The established Roman Catholic church was increasingly believed to be corrupt and overly wealthy – and its extensive lands were seen as a source of power and money by many Reforming nobles.

Henry VIII of England had renounced Papal authority, and had taken the church's wealth and lands for his own disposal. His dispute with the church was not only about doctrine – if at all: the church would not allow him to divorce his wife. Latterly, he took more direct action, and had several wives beheaded.

The teachings of Luther and Calvin had become popular in Scotland, particularly in the east, and some of those who advocated change were burnt as martyrs by the church. This had led, in part, to the murder of the Archbishop of St Andrews, Cardinal David Beaton, in 1546. He was slain at St Andrews Castle, and his dead body hung naked from one of the windows. The castle was then held by the Reformers until French aid broke their defence.

The Reformers continued to gain influence and power, led by men such as John Knox. In 1554 Mary of Guise, who supported the Roman Catholic church and the French, had herself made Regent, but in 1557 the *First Bond* was signed, in which several Reforming Earls and Lords declared their intent to overthrow the Church.

This flared into open warfare in 1559, but peace was signed between the Lords and the Regent, allowing freedom of worship. Mary of Guise died in 1560, and Mary, Queen of Scots, returned from France in 1561 after Francis, her husband, had died. At a parliament the same year it was agreed to make Scotland a Protestant country, abolishing the Latin mass and introducing a reformed Confession of Faith.

1558–60 Mary, Queen of Scots

Mary had been taken to France in 1548 when she was only six years old, and had been brought up in the French court. She was the legitimate heir to the throne of Scots; and the French believed she was the rightful Queen of England, as they considered Elizabeth of England to be illegitimate. Elizabeth was the daughter of Anne Boleyn, but Henry VIII had divorced his first wife to marry Anne, a divorce not recognised by the Catholic church.

Mary was married to Francis, the Dauphin of France in 1558 when she was 15, although it is not clear whether the marriage was ever consummated. The Dauphin, later Francis II of France, was a sickly young man, and after they had been married only two years, he died in 1560 from an ear infection. Mary returned to Scotland in 1561, although she continued to use *Stuart*, a French misspelling of *Stewart*.

1561–87 Mary returns to Scotland

Mary began her personal reign sensibly, remaining a Catholic, but allowing the church to be Protestant, although only Mary was allowed to hear Mass. She had trouble with the powerful Catholic Gordon Earl of Huntly in 1562, but her forces defeated the Earl at the Battle of Corrichie, and Huntly Castle was torched, while the Earl died reputedly from apoplexy.

Her marriage in 1565 to Henry Stewart, Lord Darnley, however, precipitated a revolt. The murder of David Rizzio – her secretary and favourite – by Darnley, and others, at Holyrood Palace, forced Mary and Darnley apart. Knox further undermined her

Holyrood Palace

position by preaching against her, after they had had a series of heated meetings.

Mary gave birth to a son, the future James VI, at Edinburgh Castle; but Darnley was strangled at Kirk o' Field in Edinburgh in 1567 after the house he had been staying in was blown up with gunpowder. Mary quickly married James Hepburn, Earl of Bothwell, who was suspected of being involved in the murder. Bothwell had apparently kidnapped the Queen, but she had previously visited him for several days at Hermitage Castle after riding the many miles from Jedburgh.

An army was raised against Mary and Bothwell, and they were defeated at the Battle of Carberry Hill. Bothwell fled Scotland, but Mary was imprisoned in Lochleven Castle, where she was forced to abdicate in favour of her young son, James VI. Mary escaped from the castle in 1568, but – although supported by the Hamiltons and Kennedys and many other families – lost the Battle of Langside. She fled Scotland in 1568, hoping for help from her cousin, Elizabeth of England, but was imprisoned when she arrived in England.

Many families still supported Mary and Edinburgh Castle was held for her until 1573, after which support withered and many of her followers were executed.

After having been found guilty of plotting against Elizabeth, Mary was eventually beheaded in 1587 at Fotheringhay Castle in England.

Regents acted during the minority of James VI: the Stewart Earl of Moray, who was murdered at Linlithgow in 1570; the Stewart Earl of Lennox, father of Darnley, who was shot and killed at Stirling; the Erskine Earl of Mar, who died in 1572; and the Douglas Earl of Morton, who was Regent until 1578, but was executed in 1581 for his suspected part in the murder of Darnley.

The University of Edinburgh was founded in 1580.

1581-1602 James VI

James VI became king in his own right in 1581, but in 1582 was kidnapped by a group of Protestant nobles, led by the Ruthven Earl of Gowrie. This became known as the *Ruthven Raid*, and the king was held at Ruthven Castle, which is now known as Huntingtower Castle.

James escaped and by 1585 had assumed control of the kingdom. He attempted to bring about conciliation

Huntingtower Castle

between the different factions of Scottish nobles, but dealt ruthlessly with those who kidnapped him. In 1600, James murdered the Earl of Gowrie and his brother, the Master of Ruthven, at Gowrie House in Perth, claiming that they had attacked him, in what was later known as the *Gowrie Conspiracy*.

James married Anne of Denmark, and had several children, including Charles, who was later king. James was also heir to the English throne while Elizabeth remained unmarried and without children.

He extended royal authority in the more distant areas of the country, although there was a Catholic rising by the Gordon Earl of Huntly, in 1594, when royal forces were defeated at the Battle of Glenlivet. The rising failed and Huntly Castle was sacked again.

Huntly Castle

James attempted to force an Episcopal church – one where he could choose the bishops – onto the reformed Scottish church. He restored some of the prosperity of the country, but he was the first king to impose regular taxation in a time of peace. During this time, much of the former abbey and church lands were parcelled out to different families.

1603 Union of Crowns of Scots & England
Elizabeth I of England died, and James VI – James I of England – succeeded to the English throne. James, and his court, moved to London, from where he governed Scotland. He returned only once, although the countries maintained separate parliaments.

1610–18 Episcopal Church restored
James finally managed to reintroduce an Episcopal church, governed by bishops

whom he could elect. He also tried to pacify the Highlands, where Catholic worship was still widespread, but without much success.

1625–40 Charles I

James VI died and was succeeded by his son, Charles I. Charles was married to Henrietta Maria, who was a Catholic, by whom he had two sons, Charles and James, as well as several other children.

Charles I did not rule well, angering many of his subjects, and his religious policy was even more Episcopalian than his father – some were worried that he would reintroduce Catholicism. The introduction of a new prayer book in 1637 caused outrage in Scotland, culminating in the signing of the *National Covenant* of 1638, asserting the right of the people to keep the Reformed church and to introduce Presbyterianism. This was followed by the Bishop's Wars of 1639-41, and an army of Covenanters occupied Newcastle. Peace was signed in 1641.

1643–49 Civil War

The Scots, again angered by Charles's behaviour in trying to restore an Episcopal Church, agreed to an alliance with the English parliament – the *Solemn League and Covenant* – on the condition that England would adopt a Presbyterian church. Civil War broke out and Charles was defeated at the Battle of Marston Moor by an army of Scots, led by David Leslie, and English, by Cromwell, in 1644.

James Graham, Marquis of Montrose, although having signed the *National Covenant*, fought for Charles, leading a brilliant campaign, and winning a string of victories – battles at Tippermuir, Aberdeen, Inverlochy, Auldearn, Alford, and Kilsyth – against the Covenanters. However, he was eventually defeated at the Battle of Philiphaugh by Leslie in 1645 – although Montrose, himself, escaped. Atrocities on both sides, including the sacking of towns and castles, and the execution of prisoners and camp followers – including women and children – made the fighting particularly bitter.

Charles surrendered to the Scots at Newark in 1646, where he was turned over the English. Despite Scottish protests, Charles I was beheaded in 1649, and Cromwell assumed control.

Excise duty was first put on whisky at a parliament in 1644.

1650–54 The Battle of Dunbar & occupation by Cromwell

Montrose raised a small army for Charles II, but his men were slaughtered at Carbisdale. A few days later Montrose was captured and taken to Edinburgh, where he was hanged.

The Scots were angry at the beheading of Charles I, and rose against the Cromwellian administration. Cromwell invaded Scotland, and his army defeated Leslie and the Scots at the Battle of Dunbar, and went on to successfully invade Scotland. The Scots, in turn, marched into England, after Charles II was crowned at Scone in 1651, but were defeated at the Battle at Worcester the same year. Charles II only narrowly escaped and fled to the Continent. The last stronghold,

Dunnottar Castle

Dunnottar Castle, fell in 1652, although the Scottish regalia was smuggled out and hidden in a nearby church until the Restoration.

Although the Scots rose again in 1654, under the Cunningham Earl of Glencairn, resistance gradually fizzled out after a crushing defeat at Inverkeithing. Cromwell remained in power, holding Scotland as no foreign army had done before, and absorbing the country into his Commonwealth.

1660–85 Restoration of Charles II & Religious Wars

Charles II was restored in 1660, after the death of Cromwell and the collapse of his Commonwealth. Charles had spent many years in exile, and was married to Catherine of Braganza, although they had no children.

Charles re-established an Episcopal church in Scotland in 1661, and was intolerant of Covenanters, who wished to pursue a Presbyterian form of worship. Persecution of the Covenanters led to the Pentland Rising of 1666, which ended in their defeat at the Battle of Rullion Green.

In 1679, after further persecution and the murder of Archbishop Sharp, the Covenanters rose again and won a small battle at Drumclog against *Bonnie Dundee*. They quickly raised an army, but were crushed by a government force under the Duke of Monmouth at Bothwell Brig.

The struggle continued, led by Richard Cameron, but his supporters, the Cameronians – who denounced the King's authority – were defeated at the battle of Airds Moss in 1680. Cameron was slain and his hands and head were hacked off to be brought before Parliament.

The years 1681–85, known as the *Killing Times*, saw further atrocities committed against the Covenanters. Not least were those by *Bonnie Dundee*,

John Graham of Claverhouse, also known as *Bloody Clavers*, although the actual number of deaths was about 100. The *Wigtown Martyrs*, two women who were tethered to a post to be drowned by the incoming tide, were two of Bonnie Dundee's victims.

1685–89 James VII

In 1685 Charles II died, and James VII, his younger brother, came to the throne at the age of 52. He was married twice: firstly to his mistress, Anne Hyde, by whom he had several children: including Mary and Anne, who both later came to the throne. When Anne Hyde died, he married the young Mary of Modena, and their children included James Francis, who became James VIII, the *Old Pretender*.

James converted to Catholicism in the 1660s, and made himself unpopular during his short reign by trying to remove any penalties for Catholic worship.

The Duke of Monmouth, Charles II's illegitimate son, rebelled against James, supported in Scotland by the Campbell Earl of Argyll, but the rebellion failed and both were executed. In 1688, however, James's English subjects rose against him and he fled abroad. William of Orange – husband of Mary, James's daughter – was invited to become king. This was confirmed in 1689 by a Scottish Convention, which had dubious legality.

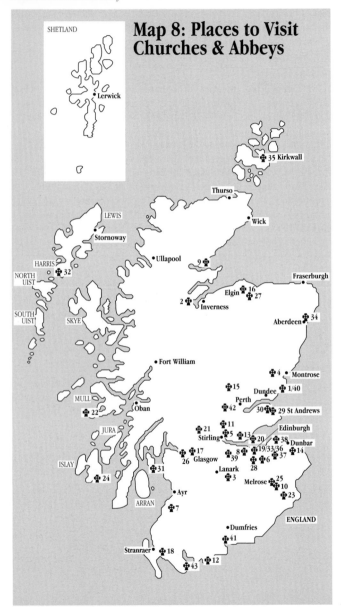

Map 8: Places to Visit
Churches & Abbeys

SHETLAND

● Lerwick

35 ✠ Kirkwall

● Thurso

● Wick

LEWIS

● Stornoway

● Ullapool

9 ✠

HARRIS ✠ 32

NORTH UIST

SOUTH UIST

SKYE

Fraserburgh

Elgin ✠ 16
2 ✠ ● Inverness   ✠ 27

Aberdeen ✠ 34

● Fort William

✠ 4 Montrose

15 ✠   Dundee ✠ 1/40
MULL
✠ 22   ● Oban   Perth
✠ 42
30 ✠✠ 29 St Andrews
21 ✠ 11 ✠
JURA   Stirling ✠ 5 13 ✠ 20 ✠ Edinburgh ✠ 38
17 ✠ 8 ✠✠ 19/33/36 Dunbar
ISLAY   26 ✠ Glasgow 39 ✠ ✠ 6 37 ✠ 14
28
✠ 31   ● Lanark ✠ 25
3 ✠   Melrose ✠✠ 10
✠ 24   ✠ 23
ARRAN   ● Ayr
✠ 7

● Dumfries
✠ 41

Stranraer ● ✠ 18
✠ 43 ✠ 12

ENGLAND

46

Places to Visit
Churches & Abbeys

1 Arbroath Abbey
NO 643413 54 HS
Off A92, in Arbroath, Angus
Substantial ruins of a Tironensian abbey,
founded in 1178 by William the Lyon. The
Declaration of Arbroath was signed here in
1320. Museum.
☎ 01241 878756—Open all year
P Nearby S £

2 Beauly Priory
NH 527465 26 HS
On A862, in Beauly, Highlands
The fine ruined church of a
Valliscaulian priory, founded in 1230.
There are some old burial slabs.
Open all year
P

3 Biggar Kirk
NT 042378 72
Off A72, Biggar, Lanarkshire
Impressive 16th-century church with a
crenellated tower, which is still used as
the parish church.
Open daily in summer
S

4 Brechin Cathedral
NO 596601 44
Off A935, Brechin, Angus
Complete medieval church with early
sculptured stone, still used as the

parish church. Adjacent is an unusual 11th-
century round tower, only two of which
survive in Scotland, the other at Abernethy.
Open all year
P Nearby S

5 Church of the Holy Rude
NS 793937 57
*Off A9, Stirling, St John Street – near
Stirling Castle*
A fine church, built in the 16th and 17th
centuries, and used for the coronation of
James VI in 1567. Still used as parish church.
Open May to September
S WC & Access

6 Crichton Collegiate Church
NT 381616 66
*Off B6367, 1.5 miles E of Gorebridge,
Midlothian*
Substantial and impressive collegiate church,
dating from 1449, with a square crenellated
tower.
Open May to September Sun 2–5 pm
P S WC & Access

Crichton Collegiate Church

47

7 Crossraguel Abbey

NS 275083   76   HS

On A77, 2 miles S of Maybole, Ayrshire

Substantial ruin of an early 13th-century Cluniac abbey, with a well-preserved gatehouse, cloister and abbot's house. Exhibition.

☎ 01655 883113—Open April to September except closed Thur PM and Fri

P S WC &

8 Dalmeny Parish Church

NT 144775   65

Off B924, Dalmeny, Lothian

A fine and largely unaltered medieval Romanesque church, founded in 12th century, dedicated to St Cuthbert.

Open May to October, Sun 2–4.30 pm. Key available from manse or post office.

S WC & Access

9 Dornoch Cathedral

NH 797896   21

Off A949, Castle Street, Dornoch

Although restored in the 19th century, much of the 13th-century cathedral of the Bishops of Caithness survives.

Open all year

S

10 Dryburgh Abbey

NT 591316   74   HS

Off B6356, Dryburgh, 5 miles SE of Melrose, Borders

A picturesque and substantial ruin, Dryburgh Abbey dates from the 12th and 13th centuries, and is where Sir Walter Scott is buried. It was founded by David I.

☎ 01835 822381—Open all year

P S WC &

11 Dunblane Cathedral

NN 782015   57   HS

Off B8033, in Dunblane, Stirlingshire.

Although restored and reroofed, the Cathedral is substantially 13th century and has some fine carving. Still used as the parish church.

☎ 01786 823338—Open all year

P Nearby S WC & Access

12 Dundrennan Abbey

NX 749475   83   HS

On A711, Dundrennan, 5 miles SE of Kirkcudbright, Dumfries and Galloway

The ruins of a Cistercian abbey founded in 1142 by David I. Parts of the church, chapter house and cloister survive.

☎ 01557 500262—Open April to September

P S &

13 Dunfermline Abbey

NT 089873   65   HS

Off A907 or A823, in Dunfermline, Fife

Site of 11th-century Benedictine monastery, founded by Margaret. The restored church dates from the 12th century, and there are ruins of the domestic buildings and 16th-century palace. Robert the Bruce is buried in the church. Exhibition.

01383 739026—Choir of church closed October to March

P Nearby S &

14 Dunglass Collegiate Church

NT 766718   67   HS

Off A1, Dunglass, 1 mile NW of Cockburnspath, East Lothian

Ruined but roofed cross-shaped church of St Mary, founded about 1450 as a college of canons, by Sir Alexander Home.

Open all year

P Nearby

15 Dunkeld Cathedral

N0 025426   53

Off A923, Dunkeld, Perthshire

Medieval church, the choir of which is used as the parish church, while the nave is ruined. Chapter house has a small museum.

Open all year

P Nearby S WC & Access

Elgin Cathedral

16 Elgin Cathedral
NJ 222632 28 HS
Off A96, Elgin, Moray
Substantial ruined cathedral, once one of the
most impressive churches in Scotland,
dating from the 13th century. Fine chapter
house. Exhibition. Grave slabs. Interesting
graveyard.
☎ 01343 547171—Open all year –
joint entry ticket Spynie Palace
 P Nearby S &

17 Glasgow Cathedral
NS 602655 64 HS
Centre of Glasgow
The present cathedral, the only medieval
cathedral in mainland Scotland to have
survived the Reformation complete, is built
over the tomb of St Mungo or Kentigern.
The building has a fine crypt and a 15th-
century stone screen.
☎ 0141 552 6891—Open all year
P Nearby 🖦 S wc & Access

18 Glenluce Abbey
NX 185586 82 HS
*Off A75, 1.5 miles N of Glenluce village,
Dumfries and Galloway*
Ruins of a Cistercian abbey dating from 1192,

the fine chapter house of which is still
roofed. Exhibition.
☎ 01581 300541—Open daily April to
September; weekends only October to
March
P S &

19 Holyrood Abbey
NT 269740 66 HS
*Edinburgh, in the grounds of
Holyroodhouse*
The ruined church of an Augustinian abbey,
founded by David I in 1128, survives beside
the palace.
See Holyrood Palace

20 Inchcolm Abbey
NT 191827 66 HS
On an island in the Firth of Forth
Very well preserved group of monastic
buildings, founded in 1123 by Alexander I.
The cloister and chapter house are
complete. Interesting island. Exhibition.
☎ 01383 823332—Closed in winter –
ferry from South Queensferry or North
Queensferry (☎ 0131 331 4857)
S wc &

21 Inchmahome Priory

NN 574005 57 HS

Off A81, island in the Lake of Menteith, Stirlingshire

Picturesque ruins of a small Augustinian priory on a wooded island. The priory was founded in 1238 by Walter Comyn, Earl of Menteith.

☎ 01877 385294—Open April to September – ferry from Port of Menteith.

P S WC &

22 Iona Abbey & Nunnery

NM 287245 48

Off A849, Island of Iona, Argyll

St Columba came here from Ireland in 563, formed a monastic community, and converted the Picts. Surviving abbey buildings date from early 13th century after it had been refounded by Queen Margaret . Although very ruined, the abbey was rebuilt in 1938 for the Iona Community. St Martin's Cross stands outside the abbey, and the museum houses splendid sculptured stones and crosses. Many of the early Kings of Scots are buried here, as well as kings of Ireland and Norway. The nearby nunnery of St Mary was founded in 1208.

Open all year – parking and ferry (&) from Fionnphort, no cars on Iona

🍵 S WC & Limited

23 Jedburgh Abbey

NT 650204 74 HS

Off A68, Jedburgh, Borders

Founded by David I about 1138 as an Augustinian abbey, much of the church and some foundations of the domestic buildings survive. Visitor centre.

☎ 01835 863925—Open all year

P 🍵 S WC & & WC/Lim access

24 Kildalton Cross and Chapel

NR 458508 60 HS

Off A846, 6.5 miles NE of Port Ellen, on Islay

The finest surviving intact High Cross in Scotland, dating from the 9th century, with a small chapel and later cross nearby.

Open all year

P Nearby

25 Melrose Abbey

NT 548341 73 HS

Off A6091, Melrose, Borders

An elegant and picturesque ruin, Melrose Abbey was founded by David I about 1136 as a Cistercian abbey. The heart of Robert the Bruce is buried here. Museum in the Abbot's house. Audio guide available.

☎ 01896 822562—Open all year

P S WC &

26 Paisley Abbey

NS 486640 64

Off A737, Paisley, Renfrewshire

The church of the abbey, founded in 1163, although substantially rebuilt, includes medieval architecture, the tombs of Marjorie, daughter of Robert the Bruce, and Robert II, and the Barochan Cross, dating from the 10th century. Used as a parish church.

Open all year – Mon to Sat

🍵 S WC

27 Pluscarden Abbey

NJ 142576 28

Off B9010, 6 miles SW of Elgin, Moray

Originally founded in 1230, the abbey was refounded and almost completely rebuilt in 1948 as a Benedictine monastery. Gregorian chants.

Open all year

P Nearby S WC & Access

28 Rosslyn Chapel

NT 275631 66

Off A701, Roslin, 6 miles S of Edinburgh, Midlothian

Richly carved but only partly completed, Rosslyn Chapel was founded in 1446 and has a fine sculpted pillar, the *Prentice Pillar*. It is dedicated to St Matthew, and many of Sinclair Earls of Roslin are buried here.

☎ 0131 440 2159—Open April to October; check winter opening

P Nearby 🍵 S WC & & Access

29 St Andrews Cathedral

NO 516166 59 HS

Off A91, St Andrews, Fife

The very ruined remains of the largest cathedral in Scotland, with St Rule's Tower. Museum of early Christian and medieval sculpture. The castle is nearby.

☎ 01334 472563—Open all year; combined ticket available for cathedral and castle

P Nearby S &

30 St Athernase Church

NO 455215 59

Off A919, Leuchars, Fife

One of the finest Norman churches in Scotland, the chancel and apse with blind arcades survive from a 12th-century church.

Open March to October

P Nearby ☕ S wc

St Athernase Church, Leuchars

31 St Blane's Church

NS 094535 63 HS

Off A844, 2 miles S of Kingarth, south of Isle of Bute

Site of Celtic monastery with 12th-century chapel.

Open all year – involves short walk

P Nearby

32 St Clement's Church

NG 047833 18 HS

On A859, Rodel, south of Isle of Harris, Western Isles

Fine 16th-century church with strong square tower and carved tomb of Alasdair Crotach MacLeod.

Open all year

P Nearby

33 St Gile's Cathedral

NT 257735 66

High Street, Edinburgh

Although there has been a church since 854, the existing complex building dates substantially from the 15th century. It has an unusual crown steeple.

Open all year

☕ S wc

34 St Machar's Cathedral

NJ 939088 38

Off A956, Old Aberdeen, N of Aberdeen

The nave and towers of this medieval cathedral are used as the parish church, while the transepts are ruined.

Open all year

S wc & Access

35 St Magnus Cathedral

HY 449112 06

Town centre, Kirkwall, Orkney

Founded in 1137, the cathedral is one of the finest in Scotland and was completed about 1500. It survived the Reformation intact.

Open all year except public hols

P Nearby S

51

St Margaret's Chapel, Edinburgh Castle

36 St Margaret's Chapel
NT 252735 66
Edinburgh Castle, Edinburgh
The oldest building in the castle, the small
chapel was built by David I in the first half of
the 12th century, and is dedicated to his
mother, Saint Margaret.
See Edinburgh Castle

37 St Mary's Church
NT 518736 66
Off A6093, Haddington, East Lothian
In a pleasant situation beside the River Tyne,
St Mary's is a substantial 14th-century
church, known as the *Lamp of Lothian*. It is
the largest parish church in Scotland.
Open April to September
P Nearby 🍴 S WC & Access

38 St Mary's Parish Church
NT 596815 67
*On A198, Whitekirk, 3.5 miles SE of North
Berwick, East Lothian*
Dating from the 12th century with a 16th-
century tower, the church was restored after
being burnt out in 1914. Whitekirk was a
place of pilgrimage in medieval times.
Open all year
P Nearby S WC

39 St Michael's Parish Church
NT 003773 65
*Off A803, Linlithgow, near the Palace, West
Lothian*
Founded in 1242 on the site of an earlier
church, St Michael's mostly dates from the
15th century, although it now has an
unfortunate added in 1964
Open all year Mon to Fri
P Nearby S

40 St Vigeans Church
NO 639429 54
*Off A933, St Vigeans, 0.5 miles N of
Arbroath, Angus*
The church dates from the 12th century,
and is dedicated to St Vigean, an Irish
saint, who died in 664. A museum of early
Christian and Pictish sculpture is housed in
cottages nearby.
Open Sun in June – other times key
available from house opposite church
main gate
P Nearby

Sweetheart Abbey

41 Sweetheart Abbey

NX 964663 84 HS

On A710, in New Abbey, 6 miles S of Dumfries, Dumfries and Galloway

Ruins of 13th-century Cistercian abbey. It was founded by Devorgilla of Galloway in memory of her husband, John Balliol – they are buried here.

📞 01387 850397—Open April to September; joint entry ticket with New Abbey Corn mill

 P **S** &

42 Tullibardine Chapel

NN 909134 58 HS

Off A823, 6 miles SE of Crieff, Perthshire

Unaltered small medieval church, founded in 1446, and one of the most complete examples of a collegiate church. Exhibition. Closed October to March

43 Whithorn Priory

NX 444403 83 HS

On A746 in Whithorn, Dumfries & Galloway

The site of a 5th-century Christian community of St Ninian. The ruins are of a 12th-century Premonstratensian priory. A fine collection of early Christian sculpture is housed in a nearby museum. Visitor centre.

📞 01988 500508—Open March to October

P Nearby & & Limited access

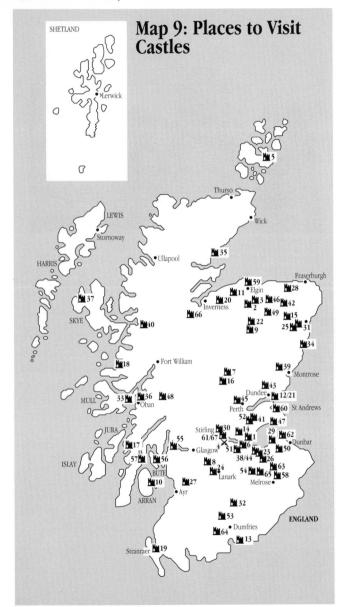

Map 9: Places to Visit
Castles

SHETLAND

•Lerwick

5

Thurso

Wick

LEWIS

Stornoway

Ullapool

35

HARRIS

Fraserburgh

59
11   Elgin   28
20   3 2 46 42
Inverness   49 15
66   22   25 31
9   34

SKYE

37

40

18   Fort William

39
7   Montrose
16

43

33 36 48   Dundee   12/21
Oban   45   60 St Andrews
Perth   52 41   47
Stirling 30   14   29 62
55   61/67   1   50
Glasgow   51 16   23   Dunbar
17   38/44   26
57 56   8   24   54 65 63 58
BUTE   Lanark   Melrose
10   27

MULL

JURA

ISLAY

ARRAN   Ayr

32

53

ENGLAND

64   •Dumfries

Stranraer   19   13

54

Places to Visit Castles

P	Parking
S	Sales Area
🍵	Refreshments
WC	Toilet
£	Admission Charge
♿	Disabled
HS	Historic Scotland
NTS	National Trust for Scot.

1 Aberdour Castle

NT 193854 66 HS

On A921, Aberdour, Fife

Large ruined castle, dating from the 14th century, held by the Douglases. Once home of the Regent Morton, who was executed in 1581. Terraced garden.

📞 01383 860519—Open all year except closed Thur PM and Fri October to March

P 🍵 **S** **WC** £ ♿ **WC**/Limited access

2 Ballindalloch Castle

NJ 178365 28

Off A95, 7.5 miles SW of Charlestown of Aberlour

Modified and extended 16th-century Z-plan tower house, home of the Macpherson-Grants, in pleasant gardens and grounds. Collection of 17th-century Spanish paintings.

📞 01807 500206—Open Easter to end September

P 🍵 **S** **WC** £ ♿ **WC**/Lim access

3 Balvenie Castle

NJ 326409 28 HS

On B975, 0.5 miles N of Dufftown

Large ruined castle, with a 13th-century curtain wall enclosing ranges of buildings, including a 16th-century palace. Held by the Comyns, Douglases, Stewarts, Innes family, and then the Duffs.

📞 01340 820121—Open April to September

P **S** £

4 Bannockburn Battlefield

NS 814917 57 NTS

Off M80/M9 at Junc 9, Bannockburn, 2 miles S of Stirling

Site of the battle of Bannockburn, where in 1314 the large army of Edward II of England was defeated by Robert the Bruce. Exhibition and heritage centre. Audio-visual presentation.

📞 01786 812664—Battlefield open all year; heritage centre open March to 23 December

P **S** **WC** £ ♿ Facilities

5 Bishop's and Earl's Palaces

HY 449111 06 HS

Near St Magnus Cathedral, Kirkwall, Orkney

The Bishop's Palace, dating from the 12th century, is an interesting ruin, the site of the death of King Haco of Norway in 1263. The adjoining ruined Earl's Palace is a fine 17th-century fortified mansion, built by Patrick Stewart, Earl of Orkney. Exhibition.

📞 01856 875461—Open April to September – combined ticket available for Orkney monuments

P Nearby **S** £

6 Blackness Castle

NT 056803 65 HS

Off B903 or B9109, Blackness, 4 miles E of Bo'ness

Dating from the 15th century, Blackness is a strong courtyard castle, with a keep, gatehouse and curtain wall. It was used as the state prison.

📞 01506 834807—Open all year except closed Thur PM and Fri October to March

P **S** **WC** £

7 Blair Castle

NN 867662   43

*Off B8079, 1 mile NW of Blair Atholl,
Perthshire*

Blair Castle, which dates from the 13th
century, is an impressive castle and mansion,
set in acres of park land. Home to the Dukes
of Atholl for nearly 800
years. Many rooms.
Collections of paintings,
arms, armour, china,
costumes and Jacobite
mementoes. Garden.

☎ 01796 481207—
Open 27 March to
October

P ▣ S wc &
& Limited access

8 Bothwell Castle

NS 688594   64 HS

*Off B7071, 1 mile S of
Uddingston, Lanarkshire*

One of the finest early
castles in Scotland,
Bothwell consists of the
remains of a round keep and large courtyard.
It was besieged several times in the Wars of
Independence.

☎ 01698 816894—Open all year
except closed Thur PM and Fri in
October to March

P S & wc

9 Braemar Castle

NO 156924   43

*On A93, 0.5 miles NE of Braemar,
Aberdeenshire*

Altered 17th-century tower house with
turrets crowning many of the corners. Home
of the Farquharsons since the 18th century.
Many interesting rooms.

☎ 01339 741224—Open Easter to end
October

P Nearby S wc &

10 Brodick Castle

NS 016378   69 NTS

Off A841, 2 miles N of Brodick, Arran

Dating from the 13th century, Brodick Castle

is a large house, which was remodelled in
the 19th century by the Hamiltons. Garden .

☎ 01770 302202—Castle open April to
October; garden and country park
open all year

P ▣ S wc & & Facilities

Brodie Castle

11 Brodie Castle

NH 980578   27 NTS

Off A96, 4.5 miles W of Forres, Moray

Brodie Castle is large 16th-century Z-plan
tower house, remodelled with additions,
although the Brodie family lived here from
the 12th century. Collection of paintings and
furniture. Garden.

☎ 01309 641371—Castle open April to
September; weekends in October;
gardens open all year

P ▣ S wc & & Facilities

12 Broughty Castle

NO 465304   54

Off A930, Broughty Ferry, Angus

The castle is a much-altered 15th-century
keep and castle, which houses a museum of
fishery and whaling, arms and armour.

☎ 01383 776121—Open Sat to Thur
summer; Mon–Thur & Sat winter

P S

13 Caerlaverock Castle

NY 026656 84 HS

Off B725, 7 miles SE of Dumfries, Dumfries

A magnificent ruin, Caerlaverock is a triangular castle of the Maxwells, with a strong gatehouse, ruined ranges of buildings, and a water-filled moat.

☎ 01387 770244—Open all year

P S wc £

14 Castle Campbell

NS 962994 58 HS

Off A91, 1 mile N of Dollar, Clackmannan

A picturesque ruin, Castle Campbell is a large castle, consisting of a 15th-century keep and courtyard. It was held by the Campbells.

☎ 01259 742408—Open all year except closed Thur PM and Fri in October to March; 0.5 miles walk

P ☕ S wc £

15 Castle Fraser

NJ 724126 38 NTS

Off A944, 6.5 miles SW of Inverurie, Aberdeenshire

From the 15th century, Castle Fraser consists of a massive keep, altered to Z-plan, with a courtyard. Home of the Fraser family from 1454. Garden.

☎ 01330 833463—Castle open Easter weekend; May to September; weekends only in October; garden open all year

P ☕ S wc £ ♿ Facilities

16 Castle Menzies

NN 837496 52

Off B846, 1.5 miles NW of Aberfeldy, Perthshire

Castle Menzies is an altered tower house, which was extended from the 16th century. It was home of the Menzies family until the early 1900s. Museum about Menzies clan.

☎ 01887 820982—Open Easter to mid-October

P ☕ S wc £ ♿ Lim Access

17 Castle Sween

NR 712789 62 HS

Off B8024, Loch Sween, 11 miles NW of Tarbert, Argyll

12th-century castle of enclosure, with a strong 15th-century keep at one corner. It was held by the MacSweens, but later passed to the Campbells.

Open all year

18 Castle Tioram

NM 663725 40

3 mile N of Acharacle in Moidart, Highland

A picturesque ruin, Castle Tioram is a 14th-century castle of enclosure of Clan Ranald, with a tower house and ranges of buildings.

19 Castle of St John

NX 061608 82

Off A77, in Stranraer town centre, Dumfries and Galloway

The castle is a much altered 16th-century L-plan tower house, built about 1511. It was used by *Bonnie Dundee* in the 17th century, and now houses a visitor centre.

☎ 01776 705088—Open Easter to mid-September Mon to Sat

P Nearby S ♿ Lim access

20 Cawdor Castle

NH 847499 27

Off B9090, 5 miles SW of Nairn, Highland

Approached by a drawbridge across a ditch, Cawdor Castle is a splendid and well preserved castle, which dates from the 14th century. It is home to the Cawdor family, and built around a holly tree. Fine flower gardens.

☎ 01667 404615—Open 1 May to 12 October

P ☕ S wc £ ♿ wc

21 Claypotts Castle

NO 452319 54 HS

Off A92, 3.5 miles E of Dundee city centre

Unusual and impressive, Claypotts Castle is a 16th-century Z-plan tower house. It was home to *Bonnie Dundee,* Graham of Claverhouse in the 17th century.

Open all year – view from exterior

P Nearby

Cawdor Castle (see previous page)

22 Corgarff Castle

NJ 255086 37 HS
*Off A939, 12 miles NW of Ballater,
Aberdeenshire*
A much-altered 16th-century tower house,
surrounded by later star-shaped
emplacements. The tower was torched in
1571, killing Margaret Campbell and 26 of
her household. Exhibition of its use as a
barracks.

📞 01975 651460—Open daily April to
September; weekends only October to
March – involves short walk
 P S ₤

23 Craigmillar Castle

NT 288709 66 HS
*Off A6095 or A68, 3 miles SE of centre of
Edinburgh*
An imposing ruin, Craigmillar Castle consists
of a 14th-century keep surrounded by
courtyards. The plot to murder Darnley, the

husband of Mary, Queen of
Scots, was hatched here.
Visitor centre.

📞 0131 661 4445—Open
all year except closed
Thur PM and Fri October
to March
 P S ₤

24 Craignethan Castle

NS 816464 72 HS
*Off A72, 4.5 miles W of
Lanark, Lanarkshire*
Built to withstand artillery,
Craignethan is a 16th-century
castle with a strong tower. It
was held by the Hamiltons,
who supported Mary, Queen
of Scots. Exhibition.

📞 01555 860364—Open
daily March to October
except Thur PM and Fri
P ☕ S wc ₤

25 Crathes Castle

NO 734968 45 NTS
*Off A93, 3 miles E of
Banchory, Aberdeenshire*
A massive 16th-century square tower house,
later altered, but retaining a profusion of
turrets and corbelling. It was owned by the
Burnetts, and the Green Room is reputedly
haunted. Gardens. Visitor centre.

📞 01330 844525—Open April to
October; grounds and gardens open
all year
P ☕ S wc ₤ ♿ wc/Lim access

26 Crichton Castle

NT 380612 66 HS
*Off B6367, 2 miles E of Gorebridge,
Midlothian*
Fine ruined courtyard castle, with a
diamond-fashioned facade, consisting of a
14th-century keep and later ranges of
buildings. It was built by the Crichtons.

📞 01875 320017—Open April to
September – 600 yard walk to castle
P S ₤

27 Dean Castle

NS 437394 70

Off B7038, 1 mile NE of Kilmarnock, Ayrshire

Splendid restored castle, dating from the 14th century, with a keep, hall block, and enclosing curtain wall. It was held by the Boyd family, who lived here for 400 years. Park. Collections of armour and musical instruments.

☎ 01563 526401—Castle open from 12 noon all year

P ⬛ S WC £ & Lim access

28 Delgatie Castle

NJ 755506 29

Off A947, 2 miles E of Turriff, Aberdeenshire

Imposing and well preserved, Delgatie Castle is an L-shaped tower house, and was held by the Hays. Its now the private home of Captain John Hay of Delgatie, and houses the Clan Hay centre.

☎ 01888 563479— Open April to October

P ⬛ S WC £
& WC/Lim access

29 Dirleton Castle

NT 518840 66 HS

Off A198, Dirleton, 2 miles W of North Berwick, Lothian

A fine ruined courtyard castle, dating from the 13th century but altered in the 14th and 16th centuries, with a gatehouse and ditch. Garden. Exhibition.

☎ 01620 850330—Open all year

P S £

30 Doune Castle

NN 731011 57 HS

Off A820, 0.25 miles SE of Doune, Stirling

Consisting of two strong 14th-century towers, joined by a lower range, with a courtyard, Doune Castle was built by Robert, Duke of Albany, and is in a picturesque location. Exhibition.

☎ 01786 841742—Open all year except closed Thur PM and Fri October to March

P S £

Doune Castle

31 Drum Castle

NJ 796005 38 NTS

Off A93, 3 miles W of Peterculter, Aberdeenshire

Drum Castle consists of a plain 13th-century keep, to which has been added ranges from the 17th century. The property was held by

the Irvines from 1323. Garden.
01330 811204—Castle open Easter weekend; May to September; weekends only in October; grounds open all year

P ➡ S ᵂᶜ £ ♿ Facilities

32 Drumlanrig Castle

NX 851992 78

Off A76, 3 miles N of Thornhill, Dumfries-shire

A magnificent 17th-century courtyard mansion, built for the Douglas family, which stands on the site of a 15th-century castle. Renowned art collection, including works by Rembrandt, Leonardo and Holbein. Gardens. Visitor centre.

☎ 01848 330248—Open early May to late August except Thur

P ➡ S ᵂᶜ £ ♿ Access

33 Duart Castle

NM 749354 49

Off A849, 3 miles SE of Craignure, Mull

Duart Castle, impressive and daunting, consists of a large 13th-century curtain wall enclosing a massive 15th-century keep and ranges of buildings. Home of the MacLeans, it became ruinous, but was restored by the family in 1911. Exhibition.

☎ 01680 812309—Open May to mid-October

P ➡ S ᵂᶜ £

Duart Castle

34 Dunnottar Castle

NO 882839 45

Off A92, 2 miles S of Stonehaven, Aberdeenshire

In a spectacular location, Dunnottar Castle is a stronghold on a promontory, with a keep, ranges of buildings and fortified entrance. It was held by the Keith Earl Marischals. Climb to castle, and back.

☎ 01569 762173—Open all year except weekends in winter, 25/26 December & 1/2 January

P £

35 Dunrobin Castle

NC 852008 17

Off A9, 1.5 miles NE of Golspie, Sutherland

A large and splendid *fairy-tale chateau*, which incorporates a remodelled 15th-century keep and a 17th-century courtyard mansion. Home of the Earls and Dukes of Sutherland from 1235. Garden. Museum.

☎ 01408 633268—Open May to October

P ➡ S ᵂᶜ £

36 Dunstaffnage Castle

NM 882344 49 HS

Off A85, 3.5 miles NE of Oban, Argyll

Dunstaffnage Castles consists of a 13th-century curtain wall enclosing an altered 16th-century gatehouse. It was built by the MacDougalls, on an earlier stronghold where the Stone of Destiny was kept from the 7th century.

☎ 01631 562465—Open April to September

P S ᵂᶜ £ ♿ ᵂᶜ

37 Dunvegan Castle

NG 247491 23

Off A850, 1 mile N of village of Dunvegan, Skye

The castle consists of a 14th-century keep, 15th-century tower, and later buildings, remodelled in the 19th century. It was

Eilean Donan Castle

home to the MacLeods from 1270, and houses the *Fairy Flag* and mementoes of Bonnie Prince Charlie. Garden. Boat trips.
☎ 01470 521206—Open daily 17 March to October
P ⬛ S ᴡᴄ £ ♿ ᴡᴄ

38 Edinburgh Castle
NT 252735 66 HS
Edinburgh
One of the strongest and most important castles in Scotland, Edinburgh Castle covers a large area and was a fortress from the earliest times, although most of the buildings are 16th century or later. The Scottish Crown Jewels are kept here, as is the huge 15th-century cannon, Mons Meg. St Margaret's Chapel dates from the 12th century. The Stone of Destiny is to be kept here from November 30 1996.
0131 225 9846—Open all year; courtesy vehicle can take visitors with disabilities to Crown Square
P ⬛ S ᴡᴄ £ ♿ Facilities

39 Edzell Castle
NO 585693 44 HS
Off B966, 6 miles N of Brechin, Angus
Home of the Lindsay Earls of Crawford from 1357 until about 1764, the castle consists of a tower house at one corner of a courtyard. Large and fine walled garden. Visitor centre.
☎ 01356 648631—Open all year except closed Thur PM and Fri October to March
P S ᴡᴄ £ ♿ ᴡᴄ/Limited access

40 Eilean Donan Castle
NG 881259 33
On A87, 8 miles E of Kyle of Lochalsh, Highland
Picturesque and impressive, Eilean Donan Castle stands on an island, and consists of a 13th-century curtain wall and 14th-century keep. The castle was bombarded in 1719 by Hanoverian frigates, and was blown up from inside. It was restored in the 19th century.
☎ 01599 555202—Open April to 1 November
P S ᴡᴄ £

41 Falkland Palace
NO 254075 59 NTS
On A912, 4 miles N of Glenrothes, Fife
A fortified but comfortable residence of the Stewart kings and queens, the gatehouse block of Falkland Palace is complete, while other ranges are ruined. It was used by James III, James IV and James V, who died here in 1542. Garden. Visitor centre. Exhibition.
☎ 01337 857397—Open April to October
P Nearby S ᴡᴄ £ ♿ Facilities

42 Fyvie Castle
NJ 764393 29 NTS
Off A947, 2 miles E of Turriff, Aberdeenshire
Fyvie Castle, dating from the 13th century, consists of several towers, built in different centuries, known as the Seton, Preston, Meldrum and Gordon Towers, after the

families who built them. Garden.

☎ 01651 891266—Castle open April to September; weekends only in October; grounds open all year

P ➤ ◼ S ⌷ ⌷ & ⌷

43 Glamis Castle

NO 387481 54

Off A928, 6 miles W of Forfar, Angus

Glamis Castle is a large 14th-century keep, modified and greatly extended in later times. It is the home of the Lyon family, Earls of Strathmore and Kinghorne, and was the childhood home of Her Majesty Queen Elizabeth the Queen Mother.

☎ 01307 840393—Open 28 March to 26 October

P ➤ ◼ S ⌷ ⌷ & ⌷/Gardens

44 Holyrood Palace

NT 269739 66

1 mile E of Edinburgh Castle

This palace, one range of which dates from the 16th century, is the official residence of the monarch in Scotland. David Rizzio, favourite of Mary, Queen of Scots, was murdered here in 1566. The ruins of the Abbey church adjoin.

☎ 0131 556 1096—Open all year except during Queen's residence

P Nearby S ⌷

45 Huntingtower Castle

NO 083252 58 HS

On A85, 2.5 miles NW of Perth

The oldest part of Huntingtower is a 15th-century keep, to which was added a 16th-century tower house, and later a joining block, all still roofed. It built by the Ruthven family, and has 16th-century wall paintings.

☎ 01738 627231—Open all year except closed Thur PM and Fri October to March

P S ⌷

46 Huntly Castle

NJ 532407 29 HS

Off A920, Huntly, Aberdeenshire

A fine building with a long and turbulent history, the substantial ruins of Huntly Castle date mostly from the 15th and 16th centuries. It was the seat of the Gordon Earls of Huntly.

☎ 01466 793191—Open all year except Thurs PM and Frid October to March

P S ⌷ ⌷

47 Kellie Castle

NO 520052 59 NTS

Off B9171, 4 miles N of Elie, Fife

A large, complex building, Kellie Castle was developed between the 14th and 17th centuries. The Oliphants held the property from 1360 until 1613. Garden. Exhibition.

☎ 01333 720271—Open Easter weekend; open May to September; open weekends only in October; grounds open all year

P ➤ ◼ S ⌷ ⌷ & Facilities.

Kellie Castle

48 Kilchurn Castle

NN 133276 50 HS

Off A85, 2 miles W of Dalmally, Argyll
Picturesque and much photographed,
Kilchurn Castle stands on a promontory in
Loch Awe and is a courtyard castle with a
keep. It dates from the 15th century, and
was built by the Campbells.

Open all year

P Nearby – involves walk

49 Kildrummy Castle

NJ 454164 37 HS

*Off A97, 1 mile SW of Kildrummy village,
Aberdeenshire*
Although now very ruinous, Kildrummy was
one of the most powerful early strongholds
in Scotland. It was captured by the English in
1296, after which Nigel Bruce, brother of
Robert the Bruce, was hanged.

☎ 01975 571331—Open April to
September

P **S** **WC** ⅃ **⅃** **WC**

50 Lennoxlove House

NT 515721 66

*Off B6369 and B6368, 1 mile S of
Haddington, East Lothian*
Dating from the 15th century or before,
Lennoxlove House incorporates a tower
house into the later work. Treasures include
the death mask of Mary, Queen of Scots, and
the casket from the *Casket Letters*.

☎ 01620 823720—Open Easter
weekend; May to September Sat, Sun
& Wed PM

P **WC** ⅃ **⅃** **WC**/Gardens only

51 Linlithgow Palace

NT 003774 65 HS

Off A803, Linlithgow, West Lothian
Once a splendid palace and still a spectacular
ruin, the Palace consists of a courtyard
surrounded by buildings. It was used by the
Stewarts, and Mary, Queen of Scots, was
born here in 1542, as was her father, James
V, in 1512.

☎ 01506 842896—Open all year

P **S** ⅃

52 Lochleven Castle

NO 138018 58 HS

Off B996, 1 mile E of Kinross, Perthshire
Standing on a small island in Loch Leven, the
castle consists of a 15th-century keep with a
small courtyard. Mary, Queen of Scots, was
imprisoned here in 1567-8, during which
time she signed her abdication, although she
later escaped.

☎ 01786 450000—Open April to
September; ferry out to island from
Kinross

P **S** **WC** ⅃ **⅃** **WC**

53 Maxwelton House

NX 822898 78

*Off A702 or B729, 2.5 miles E of Moniaive,
Dumfries*
Maxwelton House, dating from 1370 or
earlier, was completely restored in the 1970s.
It was home to the Laurie family from 1611,
and Annie Laurie, heroine of the ballad, was
born here. Museum. Gardens. Chapel.

☎ 01848 200385—Last Sun May to
September; closed Sat

P **⬤** **S** **WC** ⅃

54 Neidpath Castle

NT 236405 73

On A72, 1 mile W of Peebles, Borders
Standing on a steep bank of a river, Neidpath
Castle is a 14th-century keep with a small
courtyard. It has been home to the Frasers,
Hays, and Douglases, but was besieged by
Cromwell in 1650. Museum.

☎ 01721 720333—Open Thur before
Easter to September

P **S** ⅃ **⅃** Limited Access

55 Newark Castle

NS 331745 63 HS

Off A8, Port Glasgow, Renfrew
This fine castle consists of a 15th-century
keep, 16th-century gatehouse, and other
ranges of buildings. It was built by the
Maxwells.

☎ 01475 741858—Open April to
September

P **S** **WC** ⅃

56 Rothesay Castle

NS 086646 63 HS

Off A844, in Rothesay, Bute

Surrounded by a moat, the castle has a large courtyard with four round towers, dating from the 12th century, and a rectangular keep and gatehouse. Robert III died here in 1406.

☎ 01700 502691—Open all year except closed Thurs PM and Fri October to March

 Nearby S £

57 Skipness Castle

NR 907577 62 HS

Off B8001, Skipness, east coast of Kintyre, Argyll

Skipness Castle, dating from the 13th century, has a walled courtyard with a ruined tower house and ranges of buildings. The first castle was built by the MacSweens. Open all year

P

58 Smailholm Tower

NT 637346 74 HS

Off B6937, 5 miles W of Kelso, Borders

Smailholm Tower is a plain 16th-century tower house, with a vaulted stone roof. It was a stronghold of the Pringles, and has a collection of figures and tapestries illustrating Border history and legends.

☎ 01573 460365—Open April to September

P S £

59 Spynie Palace

NJ 231658 28 HS

Off A941, 2.5 miles N of Elgin, Moray

Built by the Bishops of Elgin, the ruins of Spynie Palace consist of a massive 15th-century keep and courtyard with square towers at the corners. The palace was last used by Bishop Falconer, who died here in 1686. Joint entry ticket with Elgin Cathedral.

☎ 01343 546358—Open daily April to September; weekends only October to March

P S WC £ & WC

60 St Andrews Castle

NO 513169 59 HS

Off A91, St Andrews, Fife

Close to the Cathedral, the castle is a very ruinous courtyard castle with the remains of the gatehouse and other towers. Cardinal Beaton was murdered here in 1546, and there are the remains of a siege mine and counter-mine. Visitor centre. Exhibition.

☎ 01334 477196—Open all year; combined ticket available for castle and cathedral

P Nearby S WC £ & WC/Lim access

Spynie Palace

61 Stirling Castle
NS 790940 57 HS
Stirling
One of the most important and powerful castles in Scotland, Stirling Castle is a courtyard castle with ranges of buildings. It was besieged by Edward I in 1304, and Mary, Queen of Scots, was crowned in the chapel here. Chapel Royal and palaces. Visitor centre. Exhibitions. Garden.

✆ 01786 450000—Open all year

P ◗ S WC £ ⅖ WC/Access

62 Tantallon Castle
NT 596851 67 HS
On A198, 3 miles E of North Berwick, East Lothian
A massive and impressive ruin, Tantallon has a huge wall of stone, a gatehouse and two corner towers, cutting off a cliff-top promontory. It was a stronghold of the Douglases, and was besieged in 1528 and in 1651.

✆ 01620 892727—Open all year except closed Thur PM and Fri October to March

P ◗ S WC £

63 Thirlestane Castle
NT 534479 73
Off A68, Lauder, Borders
Although much altered and extended in the 17th and 19th centuries, Thirlestane incorporates a 16th-century castle. It is the home of the Maitlands, Earls and then Dukes of Lauderdale. Garden. Exhibition of historical toys and Border country life.

✆ 01578 722430—Open Mon, Wed, Thur & Sun Easter-week, May, June & September PM; Open Sun to Fri July & August PM

P ◗ S WC £

64 Threave Castle
NX 739623 83 HS
Off A75, 1.5 miles W of Castle Douglas, Dumfries and Galloway
Standing on an island in the River Dee, Threave Castle is a massive 14th-century keep and courtyard. It was built by Archibald the Grim, Earl of Douglas, who died here in 1400.

✆ 01831 168512—Closed October to March; short boat trip/one mile walk

P S WC £

65 Traquair House
NT 330354 73
On B709, 1 mile S of Innerleithen, Borders
Reputedly the oldest continuously occupied house in Scotland, Traquair is a complex building, dating from as early as the 12th century. It houses a collection of mementos associated with Mary, Queen of Scots, and the Jacobites. Working 18th-century brewery. Garden & maze. Craft workshops.

✆ 01896 830323—Open daily Easter to September; open Fri, Sat & Sun only in October

P ◗ S WC £ ⅖ WC/Lim access

66 Urquhart Castle
NH 531286 26 HS
Off A82, 1.5 miles SE of Drumnadrochit, Highland
Standing on shore of Loch Ness, there has been a stronghold here from the 6th century. The castle dates from the 13th century, but was destroyed in 1691 to stop it being used by Jacobites.

✆ 01456 450551—Open all year

P S WC £

67 Wallace Monument
NS 808956 57
Off B998, 1 mile NE of Stirling Castle
Monument and exhibition about William Wallace, Scotland's national hero, who routed the English at the battle of Stirling Bridge in 1296. Spectacular views from top – 246 steps. Display, including Wallace's two-handed sword.

✆ 01786 472140—Open March to October daily; February & November weekends only

P ◗ S WC £ ⅖ WC/Lim access

Map 10: The Jacobite Risings

SHETLAND

• Lerwick

ORKNEY

• Kirkwall

Thurso

• Wick

Stornoway

Ullapool

• Dornoch

Fraserburgh

LEWIS

HARRIS

NORTH UIST

• Elgin Duff House • Peterhead
Inverness • • Fort George
✗ Culloden (1746)

SOUTH UIST

SKYE

Glenshiel
✗ (1719)
Eilean Donan

• Corgarff

Braemar •

Aberdeen •

BARRA

Glenfinnan • **Fort William**

Killiecrankie
(1689) ✗

• Montrose

• Glen Coe

• Dunkeld

• Dundee

MULL
Iona O

Oban Balquhidder •

Perth • • St Andrews

Sheriffmuir
✗ (1715)
• Stirling • Kirkcaldy Dunbar
✗ Falkirk ✗ Prestonpans (1745)
(1746) Edinburgh

JURA

Dumbarton •
Greenock •
Glasgow •

ISLAY

BUTE

• Melrose

Berwick

• Ayr
ARRAN • Culzean

ENGLAND

• Dumfries

Stranraer •

PART 3: MODERN TIMES

The Jacobite Risings

1689–90 Revolution

William and Mary were confirmed as joint rulers in Scotland in 1689.

John Graham of Claverhouse, *Bonnie Dundee*, raised a Jacobite army in support of James, and defeated a government army at the Battle of Killiecrankie. Graham, however, was mortally wounded during the fighting, and the Jacobites were frustrated besieging Perth and Dunkeld, and soon dispersed.

James landed in Ireland, but his army was defeated at the Battle of the Boyne in 1690, and he fled back to France.

1692 The Massacre of Glencoe

William offered to pardon Jacobite chiefs if they swore allegiance to him by 31 December 1691. Most chiefs took the oath by the deadline, but the chief of the MacDonalds of Glencoe was a few days late in signing, having been delayed by the weather. Deciding to make an example of the clan, William ordered *fire and sword* against the MacDonalds of Glencoe. The massacre took place on 13 February 1692, carried out by troops, commanded by the Campbells of Glenlyon, who were billeted on the MacDonalds and received their hospitality. About 40 of the clan were killed, many dying in the snow as they fled.

1695 Founding of the Bank of Scotland & the Darien Scheme

The Bank of Scotland was founded in this year, as was the *Company of Scotland Trading to Africa and the Indies*. The Scots tried to set up a colony on the isthmus of Panama in 1698. The scheme was a disaster because of disease, attacks by the Spanish, and hostility and lack of support from the English.

1694–1707 Deaths of Mary and William

Mary died in 1694 and William in 1702, after his horse stumbled on a molehill, the Jacobites thereafter toasting *the little gentleman in the velvet jacket*. As they had no children, Anne, second daughter of James VII by Anne Hyde, came to the throne. Anne was married to Prince George of Denmark, and although they had 18 children, all of them and her husband predeceased her.

1707 Union of Parliaments of Scotland & England

Despite fierce opposition in Scotland and rioting in Edinburgh, the parliaments of England and Scotland were united under the direction of Anne. This union was achieved more by bribery and coercion than by any wish of the Scots to join with the English – although some saw considerable economic advantages in sharing the wealth of England's growing empire. The last Scottish parliament did vote to keep its own church, courts and legal system. The separate kingdom of Scots ceased to exist, and was incorporated into the United Kingdom of Great Britain.

1714 Death of Queen Anne & Accession of George I

Anne died, and there being no other close Protestant heirs, George, Elector of Hanover, was asked to be king. Anne was the last Stewart monarch, although since the Union of the Crowns in 1603, the Stewarts had seldom visited Scotland, except in times of need or war. Few of them ruled well, many were motivated by greed and lust, and latterly they had shown little concern for their Scottish subjects.

George I, first of the Hanoverian monarchs, was crowned king, although he could not speak English, and had even less interest in the northern part of his kingdom. There was much discontent in Scotland, and to a lesser extent in England.

1715 Jacobite Rising

The Erskine Earl of Mar raised the standard for James VIII, son of James VII and Mary of Modena, at Braemar; but the Jacobite army was poorly led. The Jacobites were brought to battle at Sheriffmuir, after which, although indecisive, the Jacobites withdrew and disbanded. Another small army was also defeated at Preston in England.

James VIII landed at Peterhead after the battle, and although he stayed in Scotland until 1716, it was too late to make any difference, and he retreated back to France. Many of his supporters were forfeited, and lost their titles and lands.

1719 Jacobite Rising

A small army of Spaniards, numbering about 300, landed at Eilean Donan Castle, but they were soon defeated by Hanoverian forces at the Battle of Glenshiel.

Braemar Castle

1724 Building of roads

General Wade began a programme of building military roads and barracks throughout the Highlands of Scotland to enable the Hanoverian government deal effectively with any rising by the clans.

1727 Death of George I

George I died in 1727 at Hanover, and was succeeded by his son, George II. This year also saw the founding of the Royal Bank of Scotland, and the burning, at

Dornoch, of the last person found guilty of witchcraft.

1728 Birth of Robert Adam

Robert Adam was born in 1728 at Kirkcaldy into a famous family of architects, which included his father, William, and his brothers. William was responsible for much of the work at Fort George, as well as the castles of Corgarff and Braemar, and later the fine Duff House and House of Dun. Robert, and his brothers James and John, founded an architectural style based on classical designs. Robert was responsible for designing Culzean Castle and the Georgian House, Edinburgh, and there are many examples of their work throughout Scotland.

1734 Death of Rob Roy MacGregor

Rob Roy MacGregor died, and was buried at Balquhidder. He was a farmer and cattle dealer, but took part in thievery and blackmail, and was involved in the Jacobite Rising of 1715. He became a legend in his own lifetime, although he died peacefully at the ripe old age of 74.

1736 Birth of James Watt

James Watt, the pioneer of steam engines, was born in 1736 at Greenock.

1744 Golf

Although a form of golf had been played in Scotland from the 15th century, it was in 1744 that the first golf club, *the Honourable Company of Edinburgh Golfers*, was founded.

1745–46 Jacobite Rising

Bonnie Prince Charlie, the *Young Pretender*, son of James VIII and Princess Maria Clementina Sobieska, landed in Scotland and raised an army at Glenfinnan, most of it from the Highlands. His army advanced south and defeated a Hanoverian force at the Battle of Prestonpans. The Jacobites then marched into England, and got as far south as Derby, but eventually had to retreat, although in good order.

The Prince was disappointed by lack of support in England and the Scottish lowlands, and argued with his generals.

After winning the Battle of Falkirk in 1746, the Jacobites were brought to battle at Culloden Moor by the Duke of Cumberland. The Jacobites were defeated and slaughtered, and atrocities committed after the battle well earned Cumberland the title *Butcher*.

After many adventures, including a dramatic escape with help from Flora MacDonald, Charles eventually fled to France, but many of his supporters were executed and their property forfeited. The wearing of tartan and Highland dress was proscribed, and the carrying of arms forbidden. Forts were also built, such as Fort George, to accommodate garrisons for quelling any further risings.

Charlie returned to the continent a folk hero, but little in the rest of his life inspired any admiration. He began to drink and in 1760 his wife deserted him. He was forced to move to Rome, and there died at the age of 67, in 1788.

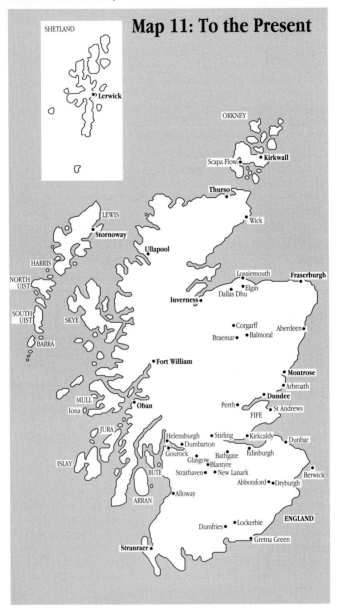

Map 11: To the Present

SHETLAND

● Lerwick

ORKNEY

Scapa Flow ● **Kirkwall**

Thurso

● Wick

LEWIS

Stornoway

Ullapool

HARRIS

NORTH UIST

SOUTH UIST

SKYE

BARRA

Lossiemouth **Fraserburgh**

● Elgin

Dallas Dhu

Inverness ●

● Corgarff   Aberdeen ●

Braemar ● ● Balmoral

● **Fort William**

MULL

Iona

● **Oban**

JURA

ISLAY

BUTE

ARRAN

● **Montrose**

● Arbroath

Perth ● **Dundee**

St Andrews

FIFE

Helensburgh ● Stirling ● Kirkcaldy

● Dumbarton ● Dunbar

Gourock Bathgate Edinburgh

Glasgow ● Blantyre

Strathaven ● New Lanark

Abbotsford ● Dryburgh

● Berwick

● Alloway

ENGLAND

Dumfries ● ● Lockerbie

Stranraer ● ● Gretna Green

To the Present

1754 Founding of the *Royal and Ancient Golf Club*
The *Royal and Ancient Golf Club* was founded at St Andrews in 1754.

1756 Birth of Sir Henry Raeburn
Raeburn was born in 1757 in Edinburgh, and became a leading portrait painter, both in Edinburgh and London. He produced about 600 portraits, some of which are on display at the National Portrait Gallery in Edinburgh, and was knighted in 1822. He died in 1823.

1757 Birth of Thomas Telford
Thomas Telford, the famous civil engineer, was born at Westerkirk in Dumfries in 1757. He was the chief engineer involved in the building of the Caledonian Canal, begun in 1804; and he built the Telford Bridge in Edinburgh, as well as harbours at Aberdeen and Wick. He died in 1834.

1759 Birth of Robert Burns
Robert Burns, Scotland's most popular poet, was born in Alloway, Ayrshire, in 1759. He was a farmer, both in Ayrshire and Dumfries, and an excise man. His poetry in Scots and English won him renown, and among his best-known poems are *For Auld Lang Syne*, *Scots Wha Hae* and *Tam o' Shanter*. He died in 1796 at Dumfries, when only 37 years old. There is a visitor centre in Dumfries devoted to Burns, and his cottages in Alloway and Dumfries are also open to the public.

1760 Death of George II & Accession of George III
George II, the last British monarch to lead an army into battle, died in 1760, and was succeeded by his son, George III.

1776 Edinburgh's New Town started
Edinburgh became very cramped, confined within the city walls and by castle hill. In 1776, land to the north of the castle was drained and cleared, and broad well-planned streets laid out, including Princes Street, George Street and Queen Street. It was to a design by James Craig. Building continued in different phases until 1840.

1770 Founding of the Clyde Trust
The Clyde Trust was founded in 1770, and was responsible for a massive programme of excavation and dredging which eventually made the River Clyde navigable as far as Glasgow. This made Glasgow a centre of trade to rival Liverpool or London.

1771 Birth of Sir Walter Scott
Walter Scott was born in 1771 in Edinburgh. He revived interest in Scottish history, encouraging George IV to come to Scotland in 1822 after the rediscovery of the Scottish regalia in 1818. Scott moved to Abbotsford in 1812, which now houses a collection of historic artefacts. Scott wrote a number of novels and

poems. He died at Abbotsford in 1832, and was buried at Dryburgh Abbey.

1776 Publication of *Wealth of Nations* & death of David Hume

Adam Smith, born in Kirkcaldy in 1723, published the influential work, the *Wealth of Nations*. David Hume, who was born in 1711, the philosopher, died this year.

1785 Founding New Lanark

New Lanark was planned in 1785, and became one of the largest and important water-powered spinning mills and a model industrial complex. Robert Owen took

New Lanark

over as manager in 1800, and introduced many enlightened social reforms, such as schools and subsidised shops.

1782

The Act proscribing Highland dress was repealed.

1790 Death of Flora MacDonald & opening of Forth–Clyde Canal

Although she had spent much of her life in Canada, Flora MacDonald returned to her native Skye, where she died in 1790.

The Forth-Clyde canal, between the two rivers, also opened this year.

1790– The Clearances

Many Highland estates were reorganized for the farming of sheep rather than crofting, and landless tenants were thrown off land they had held for generations. They left for the lowlands or went abroad, although those who left fared better than those that stayed. Lowland areas were also cleared of people to make way for improved agricultural techniques.

1811 Birth of Sir James Young Simpson
Simpson, who was born at Bathgate in 1811, pioneered the use of anaesthesia in childbirth in 1847, while professor of Midwifery at Edinburgh. He died in 1870.

1812 Launching of *The Comet*
The Comet, the first steamboat on a navigable river, was launched on the Clyde. The Clyde became famous for ship-building, after the *Vulcan* (1818), an early iron ship, and *Faerie Queen* (1831), an iron steamer, were launched here. By the 1850s, it had become the major ship-building centre. The *Queen Mary* (1934) and *Queen Elizabeth* (1939) were also built here. By the 1960s, however, ship-building was in decline.

1813 Birth of David Livingstone
David Livingstone was born at Blantyre in 1813, and later achieved fame as an African explorer. In 1834 he became a medical missionary, and travelled extensively through Africa. Livingstone *disappeared* and after some years silence, Stanley went to look for him. He found him in 1871, although Livingstone went on exploring until his death two years later.

1820 The *Radical War*
Following years of deep economic depression, a series of riots and unrest culminated in the *Radical War*, led by radical weavers. This war was in fact two small uprisings, one to seize the Carron Iron Works, near Falkirk, and another in Strathaven. Both were crushed by government forces, and the leaders were executed, while others were transported.

1820s– Whisky
Whisky had been distilled in Scotland probably from the earliest times, and had reached the Lowlands by 1500. It was first taxed in 1644, and it was henceforth illegal to produce whisky for sale. However, there were many hundreds of illicit stills. This was seen as a problem by the government, and steps were taken to prevent whisky being produced. Measures such as the placing of troops at the castles of Braemar and Corgarff were carried out in the 1830s.

 The whisky of the time was of varied quality, and turned cloudy when water was added to it. When vineyards were hit by disease, whisky began to be produced commercially after problems with consistency and colour had been overcome. Whisky is now one of Scotland's major exports, and distilleries – many of which are open to the public – throughout Scotland, produce both malt and blended whiskies

 Dallas Dhu distillery is owned by Historic Scotland and is open to the public – as are many working distilleries.

1822 George IV visits Scotland & opening of the Union Canal
George IV visited Edinburgh this year, the first monarch to do so since Charles II in the 17th century.

This year saw the opening of the Union Canal, which linked Edinburgh to the Forth-Clyde Canal at Falkirk.

1827 Birth of Joseph Lister
Joseph Lister, who was born in 1827, pioneered the use of antiseptic surgery during the 1860s while at Glasgow Royal Infirmary.

1829 Burke and Hare & body-snatching
By the 1820s, Edinburgh had become a centre of excellence for medicine and anatomy. To supply the demand for new corpses to dissect, some took to digging up newly buried bodies, and sold them to the medical school. However, Burke and Hare decided it was easier to murder to provide corpses. They were caught and although Hare turned King's evidence, Burke was hanged in 1829.

1838 Death of George IV & Accession of Queen Victoria
Queen Victoria came to the throne after the death of George IV, and she and Prince Albert first visited Scotland in 1842, and every year thereafter.

1842 Railway line between Edinburgh & Glasgow opened
The first railway line between Edinburgh and Glasgow was opened in 1842, followed by a great expansion in railways in Scotland, greatly improving transport and communications.

1843 The Disruption & forming of the Free Church
After a long-running dispute within the Church of Scotland, a large number of ministers broke away from the established church and formed the Free Church of Scotland. The Free Church is still popular in the Highlands and Islands.

1847 Birth of Alexander Graham Bell
Bell, born in Edinburgh in 1847, invented the telephone in 1876 in the USA. He died in 1922.

1850 Birth of Robert Louis Stevenson
Robert Louis Stevenson, the author who wrote *Treasure Island*, *The Strange Case of Dr Jekyll and Mr Hyde* and *Kidnapped*, was born in Edinburgh in 1850.

Balmoral Castle (see next page)

1855 Balmoral Castle
Queen Victoria and Prince Albert purchased the Balmoral Estate and built a new castle. Queen Victoria *rehabilitated* the Highlands and all things tartan, a process that Walter Scott had started.

1858 Greyfriars Bobby
When John Gray, a Midlothian farmer, died in 1858 and was buried in Greyfriars Kirkyard in Edinburgh, his terrier *Bobby* stayed by his master's grave until the dog died in 1872.

1868 Birth of Charles Rennie Mackintosh
Mackintosh was born in Glasgow, and studied at the Glasgow School of Art. He won a competition to design the new Glasgow School of Art in 1894, and his designs won him much renown. He died in 1928.

1873 Scottish Football Association founded
The Scottish Football Association was founded after a meeting of the representatives of eight clubs. Glasgow Rangers football club was also founded.

1879 Tay Bridge Disaster
The Tay Bridge, linking Dundee to Fife, collapsed as a train crossed it, killing all those aboard, reportedly around 150 people.

1880– Crofters' Rights
By the 1880s there was general discontent with the way that crofters were treated by their landlords. In 1882 this came to a head at the Battle of the Braes on Skye, when crofters defied their landlords over the introduction of sheep, and policemen from Glasgow were brought in. This forced the government to review the situation and set up a commission of inquiry. *The Crofters' Holding Act* was passed by parliament in 1886, giving crofters new rights and security of tenure.

1881 Birth of Sir Alexander Fleming
Fleming was born at Lochfield in Ayrshire in 1881, and in 1928 discovered penicillin. His discovery was not used fully until the Second World War, and he received the Nobel Prize in 1945. He died in 1955.

1886 Launching of the *Cutty Sark*
The *Cutty Sark*, the famous tea clipper, was launched at Dumbarton.

1887 Scottish Office established
The Scottish Office, which administers most of Scottish government, was established at Whitehall in London in 1887.

1888 Birth of John Logie Baird
Baird was born in Helensburgh in 1888, and built the first working television in 1929 after studying at the University of Glasgow. Baird was associated with many of the outside broadcasting advances of the 1930s. He died in 1946.
Glasgow Celtic football club was founded this year.

1890 Forth Bridge Opened

The Forth Bridge, a spectacular cantilever railway bridge, which connects Fife to Edinburgh, was opened by the Prince of Wales. It took six years to build, and was over-engineered to prevent another disaster.

1896 Glasgow underground opened

The only underground railway in Scotland, serving Glasgow, was opened in 1896, although it was not electrified until 1935.

1906 Founding of the Scottish Labour Party

The Scottish Labour Party was founded by Keir Hardie and others in 1906. In 1909 it was amalgamated into the British Labour Party.

1915 Gretna Green rail disaster

Forth Bridge

Three trains collided just outside Gretna Green, and burst into flames, killing over 200 people.

1917 Sinking of the *HMS Vanguard*

HMS Vanguard, a British warship, blew up in Scapa Flow, with the loss of 800 lives.

1919 Red Clydeside

Many years of conflict with employers and the authorities led to a period of major unrest in the shipyards of the Clyde. The workers were led by men such as Mannie Shinwell, and other socialists and communists. The unrest culminated in a riot in George Square, which took tanks to quell.

1924 Labour Prime Minister

Ramsay MacDonald, born in Lossiemouth in 1866, was named Prime Minister in 1924 and 1929-35. He was a member of the Labour Party, and an MP from 1906. He died in 1937.

1926 Post of Secretary of State for Scotland created

In the same year as the General Strike, the cabinet post of Secretary of State for Scotland was created.

1932 Founding of the Scottish National Party
The Scottish National Party was founded in 1932, and although initially it had little success, by the 1990s was a was a major player in politics.

1939 Sinking of the *Royal Oak*
The *Royal Oak*, a British warship, was sunk by a German U-boat in Scapa Flow in Orkney, with the loss of 803 lives.
  The Scottish Office was transferred to Edinburgh.

1943 Clydebank blitz
Clydebank, near Glasgow, was bombed in 1943, reducing most of the town to rubble, and killing around 1 000 people. Glasgow, Greenock, Gourock and Dumbarton were also badly hit.

1949 Scottish Covenant
A Scottish Covenant, supporting devolution, was signed by over 2.5 million Scots.

1950 Stone of Destiny taken from Westminster Abbey
The Stone of Destiny, which had been taken from Scone by Edward I, was returned to Scotland from Westminster Abbey by Scottish nationalists. It was *found* at Arbroath Abbey, and then returned to Westminster Abbey. The Stone is due to be returned to Scotland.

1961 Opening of the Forth Road Bridge
The Forth Road Bridge, linking Edinburgh to Fife, then the longest suspension bridge in Europe, was opened.

1974 Scottish National Party
In an election this year, the Scottish National Party won 11 seats.

1975 Oil
Oil was first pumped ashore from the North Sea, the industry becoming one of Britain's biggest exports, along with Scotch whisky.

1979 Referendum on a Scottish Parliament
A referendum on the setting up of a Scottish parliament was held this year. Although there was a small majority in favour, a clause meant that 40% of the total electorate, including those who did not vote, should be in favour. As only 51% of those who voted in the referendum voted for a parliament, this was well below the 40% minimum required by the clause, so this was seen as a rejection.

1989 Lockerbie Disaster
A Pan-Am Jumbo jet was blown up by a terrorist bomb, killing all those on board, and showering the town of Lockerbie with wreckage. In total, 270 people died, including several inhabitants of the town.

1998 Scottish Parliament opens & Scotland wins World Cup
Pigs seen over Edinburgh.

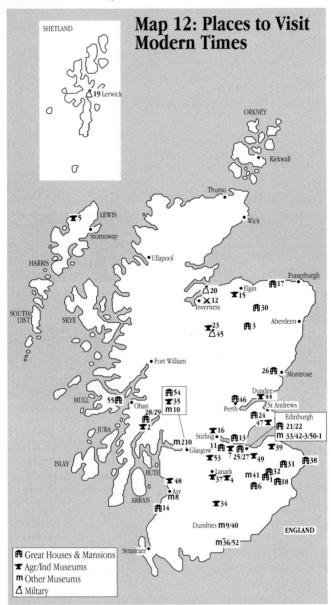

Map 12: Places to Visit
Modern Times

Places to Visit
Modern Times

P	Parking
S	Sales Area
☕	Refreshments
wc	Toilet
£	Admission Charge
♿	Disabled
HS	Historic Scotland
NTS	National Trust for Scot.

1 Abbotsford House

NT 508343 73
On B6360, 2 miles W of Melrose, Borders
The home of Sir Walter Scott from 1812 until
his death in 1832, the house dates from
1822. Impressive collection of armour and
weapons.
☎ 01896 752043—Open 3rd Mon in
March to October
P ☕ **S** wc £
♿ Access

2 Auchindrain Township

NN 032031 55
Off A83, 6 miles SW of Inveraray, Argyll
A west Highland communal
tenancy township which
has survived much as it was
built. Buildings have been
restored and furnished in
period styles to convey the
life of the Highlands in past
centuries.
☎ 01499 500235—
Open 1 April to 30 September
P ☕ **S** wc £

3 Balmoral Castle

NO 255952 44
Off A93, Balmoral, nr Ballater, Aberdeenshire
Family holiday home of the Royal Family

since Victoria and Albert bought the estate in
1852 and built the mansion. Exhibition of
paintings in ballroom & grounds only open.
☎ 01339 742471—Open May to July
P £

4 Biggar Gasworks

NT 038375 72 HS
Off A72, NW of town centre, Biggar, Lanarkshire.
Biggar Gasworks is the only surviving small
town coal-gas works in Scotland. Part of it
dates from 1839.
Open all year
P wc

5 Black House

NB 312495 08 HS
Off A858, Arnol, Lewis, Western Isles
A traditional Lewis black house, with byre,
fittings and central hearth.
☎ 01851 710395—Open all year
except closed on Sun; closed Fri
October to March
P Nearby £

Black House, Arnol

6 Bowhill

NT 426278 73
Off A708, 3 miles W of Selkirk, Borders
Home of the Duke and Duchess of
Buccleuch, Bowhill is an extensive rambling
mansion, dating mainly from 1812. Fine

collection of paintings. Audio-visual presentation. Garden and country park.

📞 01750 22204—Park open May to late summer; house open in July

🅿 ☕ Ⓢ ♿ £ ♿ Facilities

7 Bo'ness & Kinneil Railway/ Birkhill Fireclay Mine

NT 004817 65

Off A904, Bo'ness, West Lothian

Steam railway, running from Bo'ness, on the south shore of the Firth of Forth, to Birkhill Fireclay Mine. Some of the engines are over 100 years old, and the cavernous workings of the mine have 300 million year old fossils in the walls.

📞 01506 822298—Open April to mid-October (check days)

🅿 ☕ Ⓢ ♿ £

8 Burns Cottage and Museum

NS 334187 70

Off B7024, Alloway, Ayrshire

The birth place of Robert Burns, who was born in 1759, this museum contains many mementoes and manuscripts belonging to Scotland's best-known poet.

  Large museum adjacent to birthplace. New audio-visual presentation. Other nearby features include Burns Monument and Gardens, Brig o' Doon, Alloway Kirk and Tam O' Shanter Experience. Combined admission.

📞 01292 441215—Open all year except Sun in winter

🅿 ☕ Ⓢ ♿ £ ♿ Access

9 Burns House

NX 974758 84

Off A766, Burns Street, Dumfries

Robert Burns died in this house, his home during the last years of his life. Furnishings are of the period and many mementoes of the poet are on display.

📞 01387 253374—Open all year

🅿Nearby Ⓢ ♿ Limited Access

10 Burrell Collection

NS 555622 64

Off B768 or 769, Pollok Country Park, Glasgow

Viewed by millions since it was opened, the Burrell Collections consists of displays of items from the ancient world, art and pictures, ceramics and bronzes, tapestries and stained glass, weapons and armour.

📞 0141 649 7151—Open all year

🅿 ☕ Ⓢ ♿ ♿ ♿/Access

Culross (see next page)

11 Callendar House

NS 898794 65

On A803, E of Falkirk town centre

Ornate 19th-century mansion, incorporating early buildings, including a 14th-century keep. It houses a museum, and restored kitchen of the 1820s. History research centre

📞 01324 612134—Open all year

🅿 Nearby ♨ S ♿ ₤ ♿ Access/Lift

12 Culloden Battlefield

NH 743452 27 NTS

On B9006, Culloden Moor, 5 miles E of Inverness, Highland

Site of the last major battle fought on British soil in 1746, when a Jacobite army led by Bonnie Prince Charlie was crushed by a Hanoverian army, led by the Duke of Cumberland. Visitor Centre and museum. Audio-visual presentation.

📞 01463 790607—Site open all year; visitor centre open February to December except 25/26 December

🅿 ♨ S ♿ ₤ ♿ Facilities

13 Culross Palace

NS 986862 65 NTS

Off A985, Culross, Fife

The Palace was built between 1597 and 1611, and consists of ranges of gabled buildings, featuring decorative painted woodwork and original interiors. Steeply terraced garden.

📞 01383 880359—Open April to September

🅿 Nearby ♨ S ♿ ₤ ♿ Facilities

14 Culzean Castle

NS 233103 70 NTS

Off A719, 4.5 miles W of Maybole, Ayrshire.

The magnificent mansion of the Kennedy Earl of Cassillis, built between 1777-92 by the architect, Robert Adam. Collections of paintings and furniture. Country park and visitor centre – one of the foremost tourist attractions in Scotland.

📞 01655 760274—Open April to October; park open all year

🅿 ♨ S ♿ ₤ ♿ Facilities

15 Dallas Dhu Distillery

NJ 035566 27 HS

Off A940, 1 mile S of Forres, Moray

A well-preserved and interesting late 19th-century distillery with all buildings open to the public. Audio-visual presentation.

📞 01309 676548—Open all year except closed Thur PM and Fri October to March

🅿 S ♿ ₤ ♿ ♿

Duff House (see next page)

16 Doune Motor Museum

NN 716028 57

Off A84, NE of Doune, Stirlingshire

A fine collection of vintage and classic motor cars.

☎ 01786 841203—Open April to October

P ☕ S ♿ ℰ & Facilities

17 Duff House

NJ 692633 29 HS

Off A97, in Banff, Aberdeenshire

Fine early-Georgian mansion, designed by William Adam. Houses collection of paintings and other items.

☎ 01261 818181—Open all year except Tue April to September & Mon–Wed October to March

P ☕ S ♿ ℰ & Facilities inc lift

18 Floors Castle

NT 711346 74

On A6089, 1 mile NW of Kelso, Borders

The largest inhabited castle in Scotland, the house dates from 1721 and is a huge castellated mansion. Collections of furniture and porcelain. Garden and park.

☎ 01573 223333—Open Easter to September; October Sun & Wed

P ☕ S ♿ ℰ & ♿/Lift for wheelchairs/Access to house

19 Fort Charlotte

HU 475415 04 HS

Off A970, Lerwick, Shetland

A five-sided artillery fort with high and massive walls. It was first built in 1635 to protect Shetland against the Dutch, but was taken and burnt by the Dutch in 1673. It was rebuilt in 1781.

Open all year

20 Fort George

NH 763566 27 HS

Off B9006, N of village of Ardersier, Highland

A huge site and one of the most outstanding artillery fortifications in Europe, Fort George was built as a result of the Jacobite Risings, but was not completed until 1769. Museum and displays.

☎ 01667 462777—Open all year

P S ♿ ℰ & Facilities

21 Georgian House

NT 245739 66 NTS

Charlotte Square, Edinburgh

Built by Robert Adam, The Georgian House dates from the 18th century and is a fine example of architecture of the New Town of Edinburgh. Audio-visual programme.

☎ 0131 225 2160—Open April to October

P Nearby S ℰ & Facilities/Lim acc

22 Gladstone's Land

NT 255736 66 NTS

Lawnmarket (near top of Royal Mile), Edinburgh

A typical example of a 17th-century tenement building of the Old Town of Edinburgh. The house still has original painted ceilings, and reconstructed shop.

0131 226 5856—Open April to October

S & Facilities/Limited access

23 Highland Folk Museum

NH 758007 35

Off A86, Kingussie, Highland

The first folk museum to be established in Scotland (1934). The museum has an important collection of domestic, industrial and agricultural exhibits. Other features are a Lewis black house and a *click* mill.

☎ 01540 661307—Open all year except weekends in winter

P S ♿ ℰ & ♿/Access to mus

24 Hill of Tarvit Mansion house

NO 380119 59 NTS

Off A916, 2.5 miles S of Cupar, Fife

The house was virtually rebuilt in 1906 by Sir Robert Lorimer to house fine collections of paintings, furniture and porcelain. Gardens.

☎ 01334 653127—Open Easter weekend; open May to September; open weekends only in October; grounds open all year

P ☕ S ♿ ℰ & Facilities

25 Hopetoun House

NT 089790 65

Off A904, 2.5 miles W of Forth Road Bridge, West Lothian

The original house, dating from 1699, was built by William Bruce for the Hope family. Collections of furniture and pictures. Exhibitions. Park land.

☎ 0131 331 2451—Open mid-April to September

P ☕ S WC £ ♿ Facilities

26 House of Dun

N0 670598 54 NTS

Off A935, 3 miles W of Montrose, Angus

The house, dating from 1730, was built by William Adam for the Erskine family. Fine plaster work, and collections of portraits, furniture and porcelain. Garden. Steam railway some Sundays.

☎ 01674 810264—Open Easter weekend; open May to September; weekends only in October; gardens open all year

P ☕ S WC £ ♿ Facs/Grnds only

27 House of The Binns

NT 051785 65 NTS

Off A904, 3 miles NE of Linlithgow

The House of The Binns, dates partly from the early 17th century, later modified and extended. Home of the Dalyells. Park.

☎ 01506 834255—Open May to September except closed Fri; grounds open all year

P WC £

28 Inveraray Castle

NN 096093 56

Off A819 or A83, to N of Inveraray, Argyll

Inveraray Castle, begin in 1743, is a large symmetrical mansion, built for the Campbell Dukes of Argyll. Collections of weaponry, tapestries and furniture.

☎ 01499 302203—Open April to June & September to mid-October Sat to Thurs; July & August daily

P ☕ S WC £ ♿ Access to grd flr

29 Inveraray Jail

NN 096085 56

Off A83, Church Square, Inveraray, Argyll

A reconstruction of life in a 19th-century Scottish prison, including custodians in period costume, re-enacted trials, and furnished cells.

☎ 01499 302381—Open all year except 25/26 December & 1/2 January

P Nearby S WC £ ♿ WC/Lim access

30 Leith Hall

NJ 541298 37 NTS

Off B9002, 3.5 miles NE of Rhynie, Aberdeenshire

Incorporating work from the 17th century, Leith Hall is a courtyard house, modified and extended in later centuries. It was home of the Leith family. Garden.

☎ 01464 831216—Open Easter weekend; open May to September; open weekends only in October; garden open all year

P ☕ WC £ ♿ WC

Leith Hall

31 Manderston

NT 810545   74

Off A6105, 1.5 miles E of Duns, Borders
Featuring the only silver staircase in the
world, Manderston is an Edwardian mansion,
which was completely rebuilt between 1903
and 1905. Museum. Gardens.

☎ 01361 883450—Open mid-May to
September Thur & Sun; Bank Holiday
Mon end May & end August

P ☕ S wc £

32 Mellerstain

NT 648392   74

Off A6089, 5 miles E of Earlston, Borders
A fine example of a Georgian house,
designed by the Adam family, dating from

Mellerstain

1725. Collections of paintings and furniture.
Garden.

☎ 01573 410225—Open Easter
weekend; May to September daily
except Sat

P ☕ S wc £ & wc

33 Museum of Childhood

NT 265737   66

High Street, Edinburgh
The first museum in the world which
covered childhood, containing a collection
of historic toys, as well as displays on
clothing, health education and teaching.

☎ 0131 225 2424—Open all year
except Christmas and New Year

S wc & wc/Limited access

34 Museum of Lead Mining

NS 873129   78

Off B797, Wanlockhead, Dumfries
Illustrates the story of lead mining, featuring
1.5 miles of walkway past mine heads,
pumping engines, ore processing and
smelting sites.

☎ 01659 74387—Open Easter to
October

P ☕ S wc £ & wc/Museum

35 Museum of Transport

NS 565663   64

*Off A814, Kelvin Hall, 1 Bunhouse Road,
Glasgow*
Museum devoted to the history of transport
on land and sea. Exhibits include railway
engines, fire engines, cars, buses, trams,
horse-drawn vehicles.

☎ 0141 287 2720—Open all year
except 25 December and 1 January

P ☕ S wc & wc/Full access

36 New Abbey Corn Mill

NX 958663   84   HS

Off A710, New Abbey, Dumfries
A renovated water-powered mill, for grinding
oatmeal, in working order and regularly
demonstrated. Audio-visual presentation.

☎ 01387 850260—Open all year
except Thur PM & Fri October to
March; joint entry ticket Sweetheart
Abbey

P Nearby S £

37 New Lanark
NS 880425   71

Off A73, 1 miles S of Lanark, Lanarkshire
The 200-year-old cotton spinning village has been restored, and the visitor centre has an exhibition using holograms, as well as working spinning machinery. Visitor centre
📞 01555 665876—Open all year
P 🚻 **S** **wc** £ ♿ Facilities

38 Paxton House
NT 935530   74

Off B6461, 4 miles W of Berwick-upon-Tweed, Borders
Paxton House, a fine Adam mansion, was built in 1756 for the Homes of Billie. Exhibitions of pictures and furniture.
📞 01289 386291—Open Good Friday to October
P £

39 Preston Mill
NT 594779   67   NTS

Off B1407, N of East Linton, East Lothian
On one of the oldest mill sites in Scotland, this water-driven mill was last used commercially in 1957. Its machinery now provides working demonstrations.
📞 01620 860426—Open Easter weekend; open May to September; weekends only in October
P **S** **wc** £ ♿ **wc**

40 Robert Burns Centre
NX 969760   84

Off A756, Mill Road, Dumfries town centre
A museum about Robert Burns, Scotland's most popular poet, with an audio-visual interpretation and exhibition.
📞 01387 264808—Open all year
P 🚻 **S** **wc** £ ♿ **wc**/Limited access

41 Robert Smail's Printing Works
NT 335367   73   NTS

Off A72, High Street, Innerleithen, Borders
Completely restored Victorian printing works, with a reconstructed water wheel, hand typesetting and many historic items.
📞 01896 830206—Open Easter weekend; open May to September; open weekends only in October
P Nearby **S**

42 Royal Museum of Scotland
NT 255743   66

Queen Street, Edinburgh
The museum has material from prehistoric times to the present day, and the collections contain some of the most important items in the UK. The National Portrait Gallery is housed in the same building.
📞 0131 225 7534—Open all year except Christmas and New Year
P Nearby 🚻 **S** **wc** ♿ **wc**/Facilities

43 Royal Museum of Scotland
NT 258734   66

Chamber Street, Edinburgh
The museum has collection of exhibits, ranging from decorative arts, natural sciences, technology and science, and working models.
📞 0131 225 7534—Open all year except Christmas and New Year
P Nearby 🚻 **S** **wc** ♿ Facilities

44 Royal Research Ship *Discovery*
NO 408302   54

Off A92, Discovery Point, Discovery Quay, Dundee
The *Discovery* was used by Captain Scott on the Antarctic expedition of 1901-4, and built in Dundee.
📞 01382 201245—Open all year except 25/26 December & 1 January
P **S** **wc** £ ♿ **wc**/Deck/Centre

45 Ruthven Barracks
NN 764997   35   HS

Off A9, 1 mile S of Kingussie, Highland
On the site of a castle of the *Wolf of Badenoch*, the barracks here were built in 1719 following the Jacobite Rising of 1715. They were captured and burnt by Jacobites, led by Bonnie Prince Charlie, in 1746.
Open all year
P

Scone Palace

46 Scone Palace

NO 115267 58

Off A93, 2 miles N of Perth

Site of the inaugurations of the kings of Scots, the Palace mostly dates from 1804, and is home to the Earls of Mansfield. Collections of furniture, clocks and porcelain. Gardens.

☎ 01738 552300—Open mid-April to October

P ☕ S wc ﹩ ♿ wc/Facilities

47 Scottish Fisheries Museum

NO 569035 59

Off A917, Harbourhead, Anstruther, Fife

This popular maritime museum is housed in old buildings, and has exhibits relating to fishing, including painting, models and domestic items.

☎ 01333 310628—Open all year

P Nearby ☕ S wc ﹩ ♿ wc/Mus

48 Scottish Maritime Museum

NS 315385 70

Off A737, harbourside, Gottries Road, Irvine

Museum displaying maritime equipment and items. Boats include a Puffer *Spartan* and a tug *Garnock*. Operating boat slip and working class family flat. Special exhibition, Clipper ship under restoration.

☎ 01294 278283—Open April to October

P Nearby ☕ S wc ﹩ ♿ Access

86

49 Scottish Mining Museum Lady Victoria Colliery

NT 334637 66

On A7, Newtongrange, 10 miles S of Edinburgh, Midlothian

Renovated Victorian colliery, with a steam winding engine. Recreated coal face and scenes from the life of a miner. Visitor centre. Audio-visual presentation.

☎ 0131 663 7519—March to October

P ☕ S wc ﹩ ♿ wc/Lim access

50 Scottish National Portrait Gallery

NT 255743 66

Queen Street, Edinburgh

The gallery contains portraits of many famous Scots, including Mary, Queen of Scots, Jacobites, David Hume, Robert Burns, Walter Scott and many others. Artists include Raeburn, Reynolds, Gainsborough, Rodin.

☎ 0141 556 8921—Open all year except Christmas and New Year

P Nearby ☕ S wc ♿ wc/Facilities

51 Scottish Tartans Museum

NT 255738 66

Scotch House, 39/41 Princes Street, Edinburgh

The museum covers every aspect of tartan, from its development in Highland dress to the plants used for the colours.

☎ 0131 556 1252—Open all year

S

52 Shambellie House Museum of Costume

NX 960665   84

Off A710, New Abbey, 7 miles S of Dumfries

Situated in a Victorian house set in mature woodlands, each year the museum exhibits a new display of European fashionable dress from the National Costume Collection.

☎ 01387 850375—Open Easter to October

🅿 🆂 ♿ ♿ & Gardens

53 Summerlee Heritage Park

NS 729655   64

Off A89, West Canal Street, Coatbridge, Lanarkshire

The site covers the industrial heritage of the area and has exhibits including historic machinery and reconstructed houses. A working electric tramway provides transport around the site. Coal mine.

☎ 01236 431261—Open all year except 25/26 December & 1/2 January

🅿 ☕ 🆂 ♿ ♿
& ♿/Access except to mine

54 Tenement House

NS 584661   64   NTS

Off M8 or A804, 145 Buccleuch Street, nr Charing X, Glasgow

Built in 1892, this house illustrates life in Glasgow at the turn of the century, and features the furniture, furnishings and items of the family who lived there. Exhibition.

☎ 0141 333 0183—Open March to October

♿

55 Torosay Castle

NM 729353   49

Off A849, 1.5 miles SE of Craignure, Mull

Torosay Castle is a 19th-century castlellated mansion, designed by David Bryce. Unique gardens – formal terraces, Italian statue walk, and woodland. Railway.

☎ 01680 812421—Open Easter weekend & April to mid-October ; gardens open all year

🅿 ☕ 🆂 ♿ ♿ & ♿/Gardens

Index

Index of Places to Visit